Praise for

BRAND VS. WILD

and JONATHAN DAVID LEWIS

"*Brand vs. Wild* is breakthrough thinking by Jonathan, one of the more insightful business guides today."

– John Hardy, Director of Marketing & Advertising
Sourcing, The Walt Disney Company

"*Brand vs. Wild* strikes that perfect balance between powerful storytelling and practical advice. This is the modern guide to navigating disruption in the brand wilderness."

– Helen Donnelly, Executive Director, Strategy and
Communications, Verizon Enterprise Solutions

"*Brand vs. Wild* is a highly engaging read that will help all marketers properly navigate the ambiguity and change in today's brand landscape."

– Ken Yanhs, Director of Marketing,
LEGO Education

"*Brand vs. Wild* is an entertaining page-turner with valuable lessons about brand differentiation, vision and messaging embedded along the trail."

– Kevin Sullivan, former White House Communications
Director, founder, Kevin Sullivan
Communications, Inc.

"Jonathan's creativity and keen understanding of today's millennial-minded marketplace is enlightening, fun and true."

– Corey Rogers, Marketing Manager, Hyundai
Construction Equipment Americas

"Brands face forces inside and outside of their companies that threaten their survival. *Brand vs. Wild* gives you a practical survival guide that shows marketers how to navigate the wilderness."

– Kyle Martin, Director, eCommerce, Frito-Lay

BRAND VS. WILD

BRAND VS. WILD

Building Resilient Brands for
Harsh Business Environments

BY
JONATHAN DAVID LEWIS

bibliomotion
inc.

First edition published in 2017
by Bibliomotion, Inc.
711 Third Avenue New York, NY 10017, USA
2 Park Square, Milton Park, Abingdon, Oxon OX14 4RN, UK

© 2017 by Jonathan David Lewis

Bibliomotion is an imprint of Taylor & Francis Group, an informa business

FSC
www.fsc.org
MIX
Paper from
responsible sources
FSC® C014174

International Standard Book Number-13: 978-1-138-73601-6 (Hardback)
International Standard eBook Number-13: 978-1-3151-8617-7 (eBook)

Library of Congress Cataloging-in-Publication Data
Names: Lewis, Jonathan David, author.
Title: Brand vs. wild : building resilient brands for harsh business environments / Jonathan David Lewis.
Description: New York, NY : Routledge, 2017. | Includes bibliographical references and index.
Identifiers: LCCN 2016052806 (print) | LCCN 2017012081 (ebook) | ISBN 9781315186177 (ebook) | ISBN 9781138736016 (hardback : alk. paper)
Subjects: LCSH: Branding (Marketing) | Brand name products—Management. | Product management.
Classification: LCC HF5415.1255 (ebook) | LCC HF5415.1255 .L49 2017 (print) | DDC 658.8/27—dc23
LC record available at HYPERLINK "https://protect-us.mimecast.com/s/dqYaBRio6dXYUd?domain=lccn.loc.gov" https://lccn.loc.gov/2016052806

Visit the Taylor & Francis Web site at
http://www.taylorandfrancis.com

For Kellie. My love.

Contents

Acknowledgments

Any marketing and survival wisdom found in the pages of this book is only made possible by the collective courage and grit of true wilderness pioneers, men and women who trailblazed the literal and figurative wilderness so that the rest of us might follow.

It is with the deepest gratitude that I thank Steve McKee, a genuine branding pioneer and my mentor and business partner, whose groundbreaking research and subsequent books form the brilliant foundation of this work. Your shoulders are broad, and many stand taller because of you.

In the same breath, I must thank Pat Wallwork, cofounder of McKee Wallwork + Company, whose fortitude, fearlessness, and faith sustained this effort. You are an inspiration. Thank you for believing.

This book is infinitely better because of the tireless effort of my editors, publisher, and support staff. I would like to extend a special thanks to Susan Lauzau and Erika Heilman, whose wisdom and expertise were invaluable, as well as Melanie DeLorenzo and the entire team at Taylor & Francis.

Over the course of my career, I have had the privilege of working with some of the most creative and resilient professionals in the marketing industry. I'm compelled to call out my colleague Dave Ortega, whose ideas and ingenuity are reflected on every page of this book. I am equally indebted to the many colleagues and clients I have worked with over the years. Your perseverance and imagination have changed me forever, and if I've been honored to work alongside you, you've contributed to this book.

In addition to Steve McKee's seminal titles, *When Growth Stalls* and *Power Branding*, the ideas and work of a great many marketing, academic, and survival experts contributed to the development of this book. Namely, Professor John Leach, the world's leading expert in survival psychology, Colonel John Boyd, one of the greatest military minds in history, survival experts David Roberts and J. Wayne Fears, and writers and authors Nicole Krebs, Brett McKay, Candice Millard, Piers Paul Read, Sebastian Junger, Joe Kane, Dennis N. T. Perkins, and many more.

Also, to the true heroes of this book, who performed incredible feats and endured unfathomable hardship in the wilderness so that the rest of us might learn and be inspired, my utmost gratitude.

To my children, Berkeley, James, and Hazelyn (and their favorite toys, T. rex and unicorn), who missed Daddy for many nights and weekends, and to my wife, Kellie, who had to put them to bed; your patience brought this work to life and gave me strength. To my mother and father, Michael and Patricia Lewis, and my sisters and brother, who always believed; I love you.

And finally, I'd like to thank Jesus, my light in the wilderness.

Thank you.

Introduction

And they said unto Moses, Because there were no graves in Egypt, hast thou taken us away to die in the wilderness?

—Exodus 14:11

Lost. That is how I felt as I stood on advertising's biggest stage accepting two of the industry's most prestigious awards.

As I stared into the blinding lights and accepted the applause, I was overcome by the worst feeling in the world. I felt adrift. Sure, my firm had just won two incredible awards representing the culmination of our work to pioneer industry-changing start-ups and reinvigorate growth for client after client. We had just proved we were among the best in the industry. So why did I feel like I was lost in that very same industry?

Welcome to the wilderness, where nobody knows what is going on, but everyone secretly suspects someone else does. Brands are lost like never before. We blink, and everything we thought we knew has changed. Obscure start-ups usurp kingdoms. Old advantages are liabilities. And the pressure is on to figure it all out fast. The list of iconic brands humbled by today's business wilderness is long and depressing and includes Blockbuster, Compaq, Washington Mutual, Yahoo, RadioShack, and too many more.

No one is safe. Just as the ancient Israelites triumphantly won their freedom from the greatest superpower on earth then proceeded to wander in the wilderness for forty years, the most powerful brands of our life-times are a disruption away from obscurity.

And I knew how they felt.

Winning those awards would awaken me to my own firm's encroach-ing wilderness. Over the following two years, we would initiate changes in senior leadership, spearhead an ownership realignment, and pioneer creative solutions to staff and client turnover to prevent us from suc-cumbing to the wilderness.

We had faced adversity before. More than ten years earlier, we had made the Inc. 500 List of America's Fastest-Growing Companies, only to stall ourselves and suffer through nearly 100 percent staff turnover in a twenty-two-month period. That painful journey would lead to two nationwide studies into the factors that affect business growth, which became the foundation of our company's turnaround and led to our first book, *When Growth Stalls: How It Happens, Why You're Stuck, and What to Do About It*. The insights we gained would guide our company for a decade.

But now I stood in the bright lights on the biggest stage in advertising and felt lost. As I accepted awards that represented the envy of agen-cies around the world and held the proof in my hands that our approach works, I realized how disoriented I felt.

So I went back to what I had learned I could trust. In the midst of this ever-encroaching wilderness, I looked to our research. The following two-year journey would be a game changer for our firm, as we redoubled our focus on addressing the evolving challenges we and all of our clients face in the modern economy; we had to learn how to navigate unremit-ting uncertainty and change.

Titans of business and industry are falling like never before. And regardless of the security you feel today, your brand may be next. But the story doesn't have to end there. This book explores real-life stories of survival, death, and triumph in the wilderness and documents why some individuals and groups are able to survive the most dangerous environ-ments on earth while others die.

By correlating more than a decade of proprietary research with the latest in survival psychology, we were able to identify and articulate the essential qualities every survivalist and modern marketer needs to navigate today's business wilderness.

You might be tempted to dismiss the comparison of wilderness survival and modern business, but I would encourage you to think again. Contrary to the adage, business is very, very personal. Many professionals find their identity and personal value in their jobs and employers, and when things go wrong, it hurts more than the pocketbook.

Business is just as deadly as the wilderness. Researchers from Harvard and Stanford recently published a study showing that following a layoff, mortality rates rise anywhere from 44 percent to 100 percent, and reports of poor health go up 88 percent.[1] Job stress is a common risk factor associated with type 2 diabetes, heart disease, and more[2] and is thought of as the underlying cause behind up to 70 percent of visits to the family doctor.[3] You might be safer in the wilderness.

All of the stress, struggles, successes, and failures of our professional lives affect more than our day jobs. The Great Recession is linked to more than 10,000 suicides between 2007 and 2009.[4] Marriages crumble, families suffer, and friendships are neglected when work goes wrong. Like it or not, the health and security of your professional life has a dramatic impact on your well-being and relationships. And business has never been more uncertain.

Brands today must worry about endless dangers. From the smallest social media post ballooning into an online protest and the effects of terror attacks at home and abroad to cybersecurity and the next advance in artificial intelligence, disruption is the norm—and navigating it skillfully is the new strategic imperative.

The latest in survival psychology and my firm's research into the business factors that affect growth show that the very same dynamics that can kill in the wilderness are at work in all companies today. The human brain responds to the ambiguities of business in a manner that is strikingly similar to the way it approaches the uncertainties of the wilderness.

The twenty-first century is marked by the ubiquity and speed of information, reshaping the business concepts and principles we take for granted. It is no longer enough to be good at what you do. Size and longevity may be your biggest vulnerabilities. Information is cheap, talent is mobile, and today's advantage is tomorrow's weakness.

As uncertainty continues to rise, companies today are grasping to understand how to deal with ambiguity and change. This book will help. But I warn you. As you begin the journey toward building a resilient brand, you may just discover what we did in our own wilderness wandering: navigating uncertainty may be far less about the threats you face out there and far more about the threat inside.

Welcome to the wilderness. Many don't make it out alive. But some do. I'm here to tell you how.

Notes

1. Nicole Marie Richardson, "10 Ways the CEO Can Reduce Office Stress," *Inc.com*, April 30, 2010, http://www.inc.com/guides/2010/04/reduce-office-stress.html.
2. Richardson, "10 Ways the CEO Can Reduce Office Stress."
3. Ned Smith, "How Stress Impacts Your Workers' Performance," *Fox Business*, March 29, 2012, http://www.foxbusiness.com/features/2012/03/29/how-stress-impacts-your-workers-performance.html.
4. Mary Elizabeth Dallas, "Recession Linked to More than 10,000 Suicides," *CBSNews.com*, June 12, 2014, http://www.cbsnews.com/news/recession-linked-to-more-than-10000-suicides-in-north-america-europe/.

CHAPTER 1

Lost

Ruvola finally breaks out of the clouds at 9:28, only two hundred feet above the ocean. He goes into a hover and immediately calls for the ditching checklist, which prepares the crew to abandon the aircraft. They have practiced this dozens of times in training, but things are happening so fast that routines start to fall apart.

—Sebastian Junger, *The Perfect Storm*

Engulfed in the fury of a freak storm that struck without warning, the helicopter rescue crew attempting to save six men adrift off the New England coast found themselves in need of saving. While desperately searching for the seamen, the helicopter crew was forced to try to refuel in flight above a tanker in the midst of the storm. After multiple failed attempts, the pilot had a choice: continue the futile effort to connect with the tanker or race down to sea level before running out of fuel.

Sebastian Junger, author of *The Perfect Storm*, documented the spotter's experience in that moment, writing, "Throughout my career I've always managed—just barely—to keep things in control. But now, suddenly, the risk is becoming totally uncontrollable. We can't get fuel, we're going to end up in the roaring ocean."[1]

Faced with an impossible decision, the pilot pointed the nose of the helicopter toward the ocean and sped to sea level. He ordered the five-man crew to prepare to ditch in near-zero visibility. In the following chaos, both engines flamed out. The crew jumped one by one more than seventy feet to the darkness below, leaving only the pilot and flight engineer to go down with the helicopter.[2]

Humans react in a number of ways when facing a shock to the system. Dr. John Leach, professor at Lancaster University and one of the world's leading experts in survivor psychology, has spent an entire career researching and documenting the psychology of surviving. According to Leach's 10–80–10 theory, 10 percent of all survivors remain calm and retain their ability to think rationally under extreme conditions; 80 percent of survivors go into a state of shock and resignation and are unable to react to the situation; and 10 percent act irrationally, may harm themselves and the group, and are completely unprepared to cope with the new environment.[3]

The military views the resignation and shock many people exhibit in extreme situations as a product of "task saturation," an inability to perform any one task well when faced with an onslaught of critical tasks. Task saturation can affect even the best. As the highly trained helicopter crew off the New England coast found itself suddenly preparing to ditch into the storm of the century, Junger documented that the pilot slipped into Leach's bottom 90 percent: "One of the most important things on the list is for the pilot to reach down and eject his door, but Ruvola is working too hard to remove his hands from the controls . . . and the door stays on."

The problem humans face is that we are physiologically hardwired to react a certain way under intense pressure. Writing for *Outdoor Life*, Brad Fitzpatrick outlined Leach's research into the physiological process our brains and bodies go through when facing harsh and unfamiliar environments. Fitzpatrick notes that a shock to the system causes three hormones to flood the bloodstream as a reaction to the sympathetic nervous system seizing control and initiating a fight, flight, or freeze response (often called fight—flight—freeze).

As adrenaline, norepinephrine, and cortisol flow through the bloodstream, the body immediately begins burning resources to prepare for action. Pupils dilate, blood is channeled to major muscle groups, the digestive and immune systems slow down, and the limbic system takes over brain control from the frontal lobe. The cumulative result is that thoughts become, as Fitzpatrick put it, "less logical and more visceral," leading to "impulsive and irrational behavior."[4]

Worse, survivors often lose a fundamental understanding of themselves and their surroundings while in shock. The medical community calls the highest level of consciousness, what most of us enjoy every day, "alert and oriented times four." In this state, survivors know who they are, where they are, what time it is, and the event that just occurred.[5]

But as the shock to the system increases in intensity, survivors will lose basic functions of consciousness in cascading order. In extreme situations, the first level of consciousness to go is an understanding of events, followed by time, then place. According to Junger, survivors will finally lose themselves, writing, "A person who has lost all four levels of consciousness, right down to their identity, is said to be 'alert and oriented times zero.' "[6]

Survivor psychology has surprising correlations with more than a decade of research my company has conducted into the dynamics that affect business growth—and the psychological underpinnings that determine how brands react.

Every organization gets lost at some point in its life cycle. These periods of wandering in the brand wilderness are caused by major upheavals, or shocks to the system, that cannot be anticipated or controlled—and that often create entirely new paradigms for brands to navigate. According to our research, three distinct but interrelated forces are the main catalysts that cause brands to get lost in the wilderness: economic changes, aggressive competition, and disruptive industry dynamics.[7] Combined, these three forces are "The Wild" that marketers must navigate. The Wild is a storm of chaos and unceasing change that can shock even the most seasoned marketers. The difference between the top 10 percent of marketers, who respond calmly and rationally, and the bottom 90 percent, who are paralyzed and irrational, is knowledge and preparation.

The Wild cannot be anticipated, controlled, or overcome. It simply must be navigated. But those who understand the principles necessary to work with The Wild instead of against it can learn to thrive in even the harshest business environments.

Economic Changes

On November 2, 1991, the "No Name Storm" that engulfed the *Andrea Gail*, also known as the "Perfect Storm," morphed into a hurricane and wreaked havoc along the East Coast. The storm created waves 100 feet high, caused the disappearance of the crew of the *Andrea Gail*, and was eventually blamed for thirteen deaths and $200 million in damage.[8]

We all know that the economy, much like the annual storm season, is going to cycle through highs and lows. But trying to predict when and how an economic "perfect storm" is going to hit is as accurate and as helpful as guessing the next catastrophic weather event. Our research shows that the economy is the leading catalyst that causes brands to get lost in the wilderness.

Quiznos learned this lesson the hard way through the Great Recession. Already in the midst of a dramatic internal struggle with franchisees, the second-largest fast food sandwich brand was hit hard by the tumultuous economic decline and anemic recovery. Growing steadily since its inception in 1981, the Denver-based brand reached 5,000 stores nationwide in 2007 by focusing on a quick-toast concept that differentiated its product from chief competitor Subway. But as the economy fell, so too did the once-proud brand.

The recession had an outsized impact on Quiznos because many of its locations were in office buildings.[9] Franchisees also claimed that corporate kept supply costs artificially high. Combined with the Great Recession, the embattled brand faced one too many challenges and ultimately had to file for Chapter 11 bankruptcy protection.[10]

Our research makes clear that economic forces are the chief cause of a company losing its way, yet those forces remain the one thing that is completely outside a company's control. A single brand cannot influence, let alone control, the economy. Yet much of marketers' time is spent fretting or even obsessing over this very thing.

One of the lasting effects of the Great Recession is an entire generation's fundamental distrust of the foundational institutions of American society. As Millennials suffered under the weight of misguided college debt combined with the declining value of a college degree then watched the housing bubble burst, the stock market melt down, and an entire country consume itself with debt, they questioned en masse everything Boomers preached as the foundation for success.

As a Millennial myself, I had to learn to not only deal with uncertainty but to accept it as the normal way of life. The 9/11 attacks shook our foundations and began an unending, uncontrollable War on Terror that looks more like herding cats than killing bad guys. Smartphones, social media, and the always-on digital world are the reality we've known. The Great Recession hit just as many of us were entering the workforce. And our economic "recovery" looks more like a stock market bubble and a politicized numbers game than on-the-ground economic strength.

For all the negativity surrounding the Millennial generation, our great advantage is our native understanding of uncertainty. Much of what was considered strange about my generation is simply an intuitive response to ambiguity. Minimalism, renting instead of owning, the sharing economy, and more are all just concepts required to navigate constant change. In the chaos of change that has marked the formative years of the Millennial generation, we have naturally learned what most in the elder generations find so hard to comprehend: the only way to gain control is to first let go of the illusion that you have it in the first place.

The first step to navigating The Wild is to let go of the need to control the uncontrollable. Uncertainty is one of the chief laws of The Wild. It is all pervasive. It is a part of every decision, plan, and action. It is an unending companion. Yet explaining, measuring, and controlling uncertainty remains marketers' almost single-minded obsession.

In Nassim Nicholas Taleb's classic book on the topic, *The Black Swan*, the author discusses our counterproductive need to measure and control uncertainty, writing,

> This combination of low predictability and large impact makes the Black Swan a great puzzle . . . Add to this phenomenon the fact that we tend to act as if it does not exist! I don't mean just you . . . but almost all 'social scientists' who, for over a century, have operated under the false belief that their tools could measure uncertainty.[11]

Millennials naturally accept this concept. Nomadism, disloyalty, aversion to owning homes and possessions, lack of trust in the stock market and Social Security, and quick adoption of concepts like Netflix, Uber, and Airbnb all point to Millennials' natural ability to thrive in uncertainty and adopt practices required when everything we think we know may change tomorrow.

Most marketers devote the majority of their time to trying to reduce uncertainty for their superiors and stakeholders. But as risk and ambiguity continue to rise and our tools to moderate them struggle to keep up, it is helpful to remember that our principal duty isn't to reduce uncertainty but to navigate it.

Aggressive Competition

Traveling through the bitterly cold tundra near the South Pole in early 1912, Captain Robert Falcon Scott and his four companions stood aghast. After months of preparation, sailing from England across the world's most dangerous seas and marching through the harshest environment on earth, the team of seasoned explorers was standing in front of a black flag tied to a sledge bearer. The Norwegians had won the race to the South Pole. Any remaining motivation was immediately gutted from Scott's expedition.

As Scott wrote in his detailed journal of the journey, the flag, along with the sled and dog tracks "told us the whole story. The Norwegians have forestalled us and are first at the Pole. It is a terrible disappointment, and I am very sorry for my loyal companions." Thus began Scott's valiant but ultimately unsuccessful effort to retrace the expedition's route back to base camp across 800 miles of featureless wasteland.[12]

According to our research, aggressive competition is second only to economic changes in its ability to cause brands to lose their way. In today's highly commoditized world, barriers to entry are at their lowest point in history, new features can often be replicated in weeks or months, and you're just as likely to be leap-frogged by a noncompetitor as you are by a traditional player in your industry. And few note the devastating effects aggressive competition can have on team morale and motivation.

Robert Scott's failure to be the first to reach the South Pole and survive the return trip can be traced largely to hubris that led to tactical missteps and finally to a deflated and demotivated team. When planning the epic trek, Scott chose to bring only four pairs of skis for five men and scornfully dismissed the Norwegians' intentions to use dogs to traverse the inhospitable territory. Choosing instead to use horses, Scott believed he was using the more noble beast, but to his surprise, the horses could not survive in the extreme conditions and perished along the journey. Scott's decision to subsequently drag the sleds with manpower alone would be the final tactical blunder, as his team failed by mere days to be the first to reach the South Pole.[13]

If losing the race to the South Pole wasn't enough, the demoralizing effects of the defeat would lead to the untimely death of Scott and his companions. Remarking about the loss and daunting journey, Scott made one last journal entry before embarking on the doomed return trip, writing, "Great God! this is an awful place and terrible enough for us to have laboured to it without the reward of priority. . . . Now for the run home and a desperate struggle. I wonder if we can do it."[14]

Just as historians trace Scott's epic failure to pride in the face of skillful competition, many of us associate the economic, competitive, and industry forces that cause brands to wander in the wilderness with major negative upheavals like recessions and disruptive technology. But not all catalysts are negative.

Kmart, the once-proud king of the low-cost retailer hill, experienced firsthand how success and its subsequent blinding hubris can sow the seeds of decline and create an opening for competitors. By the end of the 1970s, Kmart was the dominant industry player. The company enjoyed a twenty-year growth period alongside competitors Target and Walmart (both founded in 1961, the same year Kmart opened its first store in Detroit) and even won the adoration and envy of industry titans like Sam Walton.[15]

But what began as a case study in superior business practices ended with Kmart outmaneuvered by focused and aggressive competition. Similar to Scott's tactical missteps rooted in pride, at the height of Kmart's success in the mid 1980s and early 1990s, the retailer took its eye off the discount retail category and began binge-buying brands like Borders and OfficeMax.[16] Drunk on the misguided strategy of growth by acquisition, Kmart gave highly focused and differentiated competitors Walmart and Target the opening they needed. In just a few short years, Kmart drifted toward irrelevance, while Target captured the cheap chic niche and Walmart owned the low-cost space.

Describing Kmart's surprising decline, E. J. Schultz wrote in *Ad Age* that "Analysts point to a series of missteps that date back years, from a failure to upgrade stores to a lack of clear positioning in a market dominated by Target, Walmart and upstart dollar stores."[17] In a competitive environment under assault by online retailers and entrenched with highly differentiated brick-and-mortar players, Kmart is in its last throes. Under new ownership following its 2003 bankruptcy, the struggling company continues to drift as bold competitors fight tooth and nail for the changing discount retail category.

Sid Doolittle, retired founder of McMillanDoolittle, a retail consulting firm in Chicago, summed up Kmart's lack of differentiation when he said, "Long term, retailers have to have a reason for existence that customers love. What do you love about Kmart? . . . There's nothing really."[18]

Time will tell if Kmart can find a way to differentiate and navigate aggressive competition or if it is simply nearing the end of its doomed eight-hundred-mile journey to base camp.

Disruptive Industry Dynamics

The thick, overgrown jungle valley floor swallowed the burning wreckage of the C-47 Skytrain like it was a drop in the ocean. Of the twenty-four WWII servicemen and -women who decided to go on a sight-seeing trip deep in the Dutch New Guinea jungle that morning, only three had managed to drag themselves from the wreckage and survive the following two nights.

The survivors were compelled to move. Although they were surrounded by lush greenery, they had almost no supplies or knowledge of the jungle and knew starvation was near. Combined with severe burns that covered much of the survivors' bodies and a pervasive jungle canopy that hid the group from rescue, they had no choice.

The trio set out to search for a rare clearing in the jungle floor. It didn't take long for the jungle to unleash its fury. The thick branches and vines created a nearly impassable tapestry. When the group found a stream, they desperately followed the natural jungle trail. But humidity, water, and mud do not mix well with open, weeping burn wounds. Infection set in on two of the three survivors. After two days of hiking through water and sleeping in mud, the drenched, dying trio clawed their way into a clearing just in time for a B-17 sent by the American military to locate the desperate group. They had been spotted. Rescue was sure to come. Elated, they collapsed to the ground in relief.

And that's when they heard it. As author Mitchell Zuckoff put it in *Lost in Shangri-La,* "the jungle came alive. They heard the sounds they'd thought were the yaps and barks of a faraway pack of dogs . . . the sounds grew closer. The creatures making them were human."[19] In a moment, the survivors' entire paradigm shifted as dozens of "nearly naked black men, their eyes shining, their bodies glistening with soot and pig grease, their hands filled with adzes made from wood and sharpened stone, emerged from behind the curtain of leaves."[20]

Anticipating a quick rescue, the trio instead found itself surrounded by one of the last remaining primitive warrior tribes—alarmed, angry, and returning from a large pitched battle, the warriors prepared to attack the strange white aliens—it was the natives' first encounter with modern civilization.

Much like the Shangri-La trio who hiked for several hellish days to what they thought was safety only to watch their entire context of survival change, our research revealed that the third external force that causes brands to lose their way is disruptive industry dynamics.

My firm found that lost brands were more than three times more likely than healthy companies to report that the marketplace had changed and they no longer knew their place in it.[21] Marketers today must deal with ceaseless marketplace shifts, and looking back over a century of disruption, the pace is only quickening. Ford's innovations destroyed and reinvented multiple industries and vocations. The 1950s highway infrastructure leveled entire communities and displaced countless lives. Computing, automation, and robotics have destroyed and birthed unending numbers of companies and ventures. The Internet changed the world. Smartphones changed our lives. And social media changed the game.

Everyone is affected by perpetual marketplace change. Disruption is the norm in every category and industry today. Change that used to take a decade takes a year. And what used to take a year takes days. More subtle and deceptive, and thus more dangerous than the other two dynamics, shifts in the marketplace rarely attack like a silverback gorilla but slither in like a silent snake. And the shock such shifts create can be as numbing as venom.

What the trio of survivors in the dense jungle of Dutch New Guinea didn't know was that hundreds of natives had been tracking their movements from the moment they had crashed days before. What the Americans believed was just another set of noises in the cacophony of the jungle were instead the communications of warriors stalking a new and otherworldly danger. And with just a little knowledge and observation, the survivors could have noticed the subtle jungle paths, the unnatural yaps and barks, and the crowd of eyes watching their every move.[22]

Through artful negotiation and quick-witted leadership, the Shangri-La survivors convinced the warriors that they were more a strange novelty than an immediate threat. Over the next days and weeks, the trio were able to hold off attack until paratroopers could arrive to offer physical protection. What the survivors didn't know was that their arrival sparked an intense internal battle among the warrior tribes over whether to attack or endure the strange newcomers. Weeks later, the Americans would escape the jungle valley just in time to avoid open battle.

RadioShack's disruption, on the other hand, proved to be too much for the meandering brand. The nearly hundred-year-old company had what most marketers spend their entire existence chasing: a long, deeply rooted legacy, a large marketing budget, a renowned brand with built-in goodwill, and a national footprint 4,000 locations strong.

But even the best brands can be caught off guard by subtle changes in the marketplace. Beginning with a shift in electronics favoring big-box stores like Best Buy, RadioShack fell behind as it struggled to keep up with the purchasing power and convenience of new players in the industry. The lack of foresight and urgency would lead to a round of massive layoffs and store closures. But just as the once-powerful brand plugged the leaks from the big-box electronics retail trend, online retailers led by Amazon began to suck the air out of the industry.

RadioShack hadn't changed. It was still the local, friendly, and charming electronics store everyone's grandfather used to go to. But the marketplace had shifted beneath its feet. In a desperate attempt to reposition, the brand updated stores and renamed the company "The Shack" in 2009. The effort was quickly abandoned as too little, too late. And in 2015, saddled with $1 billion in debt, RadioShack filed for bankruptcy, making complete the sad humiliation of a once-formidable American brand.[23]

Rescuers in Need of Rescue

The fierce winds of the Perfect Storm rocked the hovering craft as John Spillane, one of the helicopter crew's pararescuers, dropped seventy feet into blackness and hit the enormous ocean waves like a rock on concrete. Upon impact, he blacked out, cracked several ribs, fractured bones in his arm and leg, and ruptured a kidney. He awoke in excruciating pain and managed to find and hold on to something that had fallen from the helicopter.

Miraculously, Dave Ruvola, the pilot, managed to disengage the helicopter door after crashing into the ocean, and he swam to the surface. He spotted flight engineer Jim Mioli, who was also able to escape the sinking helicopter, and with great effort the two tied themselves together. In the frantic preparation to ditch the helicopter, Mioli had failed to put on a survival suit and was now floating in the ice-cold New England waters with no protection.

Hours went by before Spillane spotted Ruvola and Mioli in the middle of the furious ocean. He didn't believe he would make it through the night but eventually convinced himself that survival was more likely in a group. It took hours, but Spillane made the agonizing swim to Ruvola and Mioli, where the three crew members linked up and prayed for rescue.

Against all odds, a fighter jet sent to search for the crew spotted a strobe appearing and disappearing behind giant waves and called in the coordinates. The *Tamaroa*, the closest ship available, set out to attempt a rescue. With extreme risk to the lives of the ship's crew, the *Tamaroa* fought prevailing winds and mountainous waves to narrowly save not only Spillane, Ruvola, and Mioli, but a fourth helicopter crew member found a distance away. Only the fifth and best-trained crew member who leapt from the helicopter, Rick Smith, was still missing. Despite a massive nine-day search, his body was never recovered.[24]

One of the most important steps in navigating economic changes, aggressive competition, and industry disruption is to accept that sooner or later, you and your brand will be lost in the wilderness. And just like the helicopter crew in the Perfect Storm, even the best-trained, most experienced professionals are at the mercy of The Wild.

Life is cyclical. Every one of the world's greatest powers, institutions, and organizations has found itself lost in the wilderness. And as Leach's survivor research reveals, 90 percent are ill equipped to navigate it. The only difference between a brand that is lost and dies and one that survives is in the preparation, knowledge, and internal health of its team. When your brand's stress test comes—and it will—the vulnerabilities that were hidden or ignored when living was easy will be suddenly revealed.

While you can't guess exactly when you will face The Wild, the decisions and preparations you make now will determine whether you can survive or even thrive in the brand wilderness.

Survival Tips for Practical Application

Whether your brand is lost or preparing for the next challenge, it is never too late to begin the journey toward resilience.

Keep in Mind

- Three forces cause brands to lose their way: economic changes, aggressive competition, and disruptive industry dynamics.
- The natural physiological reaction to stressful environments is fight, flight, or freeze, releasing hormones into the body that lead to "less logical and more visceral . . . impulsive and irrational behavior."
- Leach's 10–80–10 theory states that only 10 percent of people in extreme environments react calmly and rationally.

Survival Tips

To navigate The Wild:

- Accept that at some point, every brand gets lost in the wilderness.
- Let go of the illusion of control.
- Focus on navigating risk instead of trying to measure or reduce it.

Notes

1. Sebastian Junger, *The Perfect Storm: A True Story of Men Against the Sea* (New York: W. W. Norton & Company, 2009), 183.
2. Junger, *The Perfect Storm*, 183–186.
3. Ben Sherwood, "What It Takes to Survive a Crisis," *Newsweek.com*, January 23, 2009, http://www.newsweek.com/what-it-takes-survive-crisis-78207.
4. Brad Fitzpatrick, "Your Brain on Survival: Here's What Happens When the Body Shifts into Survival Mode, and How You Can Stay in Control," *Outdoor Life*, 223, no. 3 (April 2016), 47.
5. Ken Giuffre, comment on "Medicine and Healthcare: What Does 'alert and Oriented X4' Mean?" *Quora*, August 2016, https://www.quora.com/Medicine-and-Healthcare-What-does-alert-and-oriented-x4-mean.
6. Junger, *The Perfect Storm*, 188.
7. Steve McKee, *When Growth Stalls: How It Happens, Why You're Stuck, and What to Do about It* (San Francisco: Jossey-Bass, 2009), 24.
8. History.com Staff, "Perfect Storm Hits North Atlantic," *History.com*, 2009, accessed July 10, 2016, http://www.history.com/this-day-in-history/perfect-storm-hits-north-atlantic.
9. Ed Sealover, "Quiznos Leaves Bankruptcy Protection with New Financial Structure," *Denver Business Journal*, July 1, 2014, http://www.bizjournals.com/denver/news/2014/07/01/quiznos-leaves-bankruptcy-protection-with-new.html.
10. Karsten Strauss, "Is Quiznos Toast?" *Forbes*, June 17, 2015, http://www.forbes.com/sites/karstenstrauss/2015/06/17/is-quiznos-toast/2/#6e9bf9bb66be.
11. Nassim Nicholas Taleb, "The Black Swan: The Impact of the Highly Improbable," *The New York Times*, April 22, 2007, http://www.nytimes.com/2007/04/22/books/chapters/0422-1st-tale.html?_r=0.

12. Robert Falcon Scott, *Journals: Captain Scott's Last Expedition*, ed. Max Jones (Oxford: Oxford University Press, 2006), 376.

13. "Doomed Expedition to the South Pole, 1912," *EyeWitnesstoHistory.com*, 1999, accessed August 4, 2016, http://www.eyewitnesstohistory.com/scott.htm; "Scott of the Antarctic (1868–1912)," *BBC*, accessed July 17, 2016, http://www.bbc.co.uk/history/historic_figures/scott_of_antarctic.shtml; Robin McKie, "Scott of the Antarctic: The Lies That Doomed His Race to the Pole," *The Guardian*, September 24, 2011, http://www.theguardian.com/uk/2011/sep/24/scott-antarctic-lies-race-pole.

14. Scott, *Journals: Captain Scott's Last Expedition*, 376–377.

15. E. J. Schultz, "Why Kmart Lost the Attention of Discount Shoppers: In a World Where Rivals Can Match or Exceed Its Price Promise, Kmart's Brand Meaning Has Lost Its Relevance," *Advertising Age*, March 19, 2012, http://adage.com/article/news/kmart-lost-attention-discount-shoppers/233369/.

16. Schultz, "Why Kmart Lost the Attention of Discount Shoppers."

17. Schultz, "Why Kmart Lost the Attention of Discount Shoppers."

18. Schultz, "Why Kmart Lost the Attention of Discount Shoppers."

19. Mitchell Zuckoff, *Lost in Shangri: La: A True Story of Survival, Adventure, and the Most Incredible Rescue Mission of World War II* (New York: Harper Collins, 2011), 102.

20. Zuckoff, *Lost in Shangri-La*, 103.

21. McKee, *When Growth Stalls*, 34.

22. Zuckoff, *Lost in Shangri-La*, 100.

23. Laura Northrup, "Judge Approves Final Plan for Radio Shack Bankruptcy," *Consumerist.com*, October 1, 2015, https://consumerist.com/2015/10/01/judge-approves-final-plan-for-radioshack-bankruptcy/; Ashley Rodriguez, "RadioShack Prepares to Sell Stores to Sprint in Bankruptcy Deal: Companies May Co-Brand the Stores," *Advertising Age*, February 2, 2015, http://adage.com/article/cmo-strategy/radioshack-prepares-sell-stores-sprint/296651/; Kevin Singer, "The RadioShack Name: Worthless or Worthwhile? RadioShack Brand Name Could Play a Key Role in the Company's Revival," *Advertising Age*, April 17, 2015, http://adage.com/article/guest-columnists/radioshack-worthless-worthwhile/298048/.

24. Junger, *The Perfect Storm*, 209.

CHAPTER 2

Afraid

Below us lay three bad rapids, a short stretch of calm water, and then, where the gorge suddenly narrowed, a single, twenty-foot-wide chute through which the whole frustrated Apurimac poured in unheeding rage. The river was whipped so white over the next half mile that it looked like a snowfield. The thrashing cascades raised a dense mist, rendering the dark canyon cold and clammy. Their roar made my head ache.[1]

—Joe Kane, *Running the Amazon*

Joe Kane clung to the cliff wall because his life depended on it. The towering river rocks were slippery and wet, and the sheer climb was more than he expected. Untrained and out of his depth, Kane did the worst thing possible in that moment; he looked down. The deafening roar of the raging river below and the instant death it offered shook Kane to his core.

So he froze. His body took over as his conscious mind shut down. He could not order his limbs to move, yet they shook uncontrollably. In *Running the Amazon*, Joe Kane wrote that he "quickly developed what rock climbers call 'sewing-machine legs,' an uncontrollable, fear-induced, pistonlike shaking."[2] Although mere feet from his companions, he felt isolated and alone. With death below and danger above, Kane's life literally hung in the balance.

Joe Kane joined the ambitious Amazon Source to Sea Expedition more out of a sense of adventure than because he had any sort of expertise. The

1985 expedition, filled with world-renowned white-water experts and a film crew, sought to be the first to make a complete descent of the formidable Amazon River.

Kane was a writer by trade and was invited because of his ability to document and publicize the expedition. What he thought would be a difficult but enjoyable excursion turned into an epic journey fraught with debilitating team conflict and an ever-growing, pervasive fear of the river.

Fear is a fundamental emotion in the human experience, driving many of the decisions made in life and business today. Yet it remains a mysterious and often deceptive companion.

Our research reveals that paralyzing fear is the first reaction when brands are lost in the wilderness. Lost brands are statistically more likely to avoid risk, resist change, and be reluctant to invest. In short, a lost brand is a scared brand. After the initial shock induced by economic changes, aggressive competition, or disruptive industry dynamics, marketers face overwhelming fear. In order to overcome it, one must first understand its power.

The basic human response to fear is a unique combination of the physiological and the psychological. Humans share a common physiological response to fear, but psychologically, our reactions are unique.[3] This means that while you must understand and prepare for the common physiological reactions you and your team will experience when your brand is confronted with fear, your psychological reactions will be entirely dependent on your organization's culture, shared experiences, and idiosyncrasies.

As outlined in the previous chapter, shock and subsequent fear cause the sympathetic nervous system to kick into high gear and release three key hormones into the body that elicit the fight-flight-freeze response. Essentially, your body is jacked up and ready for action (or inaction, depending on where you and your organization fall in Leach's 10–80–10 theory).

Biochemically, your response is fixed. Your body is primed, and your brain accesses a primal region that is more visceral and irrational. Ultimately, the valuable resources used to ready the body for action are burned up, and the initial rush is followed by a crash that includes extreme fatigue and a drop in body temperature.

This biological response to fear is important to note as you face marketing challenges that elicit automatic, subconscious, and often irrational reactions. These challenges can be as minor as being confronted with a new idea or as immense as an unanticipated technology or new competitor that represents an existential threat.

As human beings, our first reaction to an unfamiliar threat will be fear, and our biological response is rigged to make us irrational and erratic. This means that when you first face the power of The Wild, your initial reaction is probably not the right reaction, making the old adage encouraging us to "sleep on it" not only good advice but sound science.

Joe Kane experienced this classic fear response while clinging to that slippery Amazon River cliff. As he looked down at the raging river below, his fight-flight-freeze response kicked in, initiating the sewing-machine-leg phenomenon that left him shaking and clinging to the wall.

Photography giant Kodak looked down at its own "raging river" in the form of digital photography at the turn of the century. And froze.

Kodak had long dominated the photography industry, garnering as much as 90 percent of the film market by 1996, employing as many as 140,000 people, and enjoying the fourth-most-valuable brand in the United States, just behind Coca-Cola, Disney, and McDonald's.[4] But by 2012, Kodak filed for bankruptcy, a shell of its former self. How could an American icon with an employee base larger than most countries' standing armies and nearly unlimited resources at its disposal fall so far so fast? Fear.

Kodak's first experience with "sewing-machine legs" began with a bit of irony, as it created the very thing that would lead to its demise. In 1975, a talented Kodak engineer named Steve Sasson invented the world's first digital camera. The camera, which would turn out to be a transformative technology, was understandably initially viewed with fear. While Kodak was known for its cameras, the company's largest, most profitable source of revenue was film, which enjoyed close to 70 percent gross margins.[5]

As former Kodak CEO George Fisher put it, Kodak's management "regarded digital photography as the enemy, an evil juggernaut that would kill the chemical-based film and paper business that fueled Kodak's sales and profits for decades."[6] Steve Sasson, the man who invented digital photography, summed up Kodak's fear response when he recounted the first time he presented the technology to leadership, saying, "it was film-less photography, so management's reaction was, 'that's cute—but don't tell anyone about it.' "[7]

Describing the technology as disruptive is an understatement. A camera that requires no film represented an existential threat to the company. As Kodak watched the birth of its own disruption, the subtle power of fear crept through the entire organization.

The Roots of Fear

Joe Kane survived the treacherous climb above the Amazon River and briefly believed the worst was over. But he was wrong. With each passing day, the rapids grew fiercer and the river more unpredictable. As the challenge grew, so did Kane's fear.

Facing a particularly difficult rapid, Kane's confidence was nearly broken. The expedition scouted the worrisome rapid for more than an hour before taking the plunge. Once the team entered the river, the force of the water pushed them through in only thirty seconds. Kane wrote in his journal that "something happened to me in that half minute." He was thrown from the raft and pulled under by the incredible power of the undertow but at the last second barely avoided drowning by catching a nearby net. What his companions thought was an expert maneuver Kane privately considered sheer luck, noting, "I suspected I was beginning to crack."[8]

Kane tried to distract himself by journaling but found the fear of the river creeping through his mind. Acknowledging his self-doubt, Kane observed, "I had always assumed . . . that the one thing I had control over was my nerve, my ability to act under pressure. Now I wondered if I had misled myself."[9]

What Kane was developing was a memory trigger based on an unconscious association between the river and his ongoing fear of losing control. Once a memory trigger is formed, it takes incredible willpower to overcome.

Perhaps even more interesting (or terrifying) than our physiological response to fear is the process in which fear is formed in the first place—and the understanding that the triggers that will initiate a fear response are already in our brains and completely out of our control.

Fear is formed in fascinating and well-documented ways. Much like classical conditioning responses, which physiologist Ivan Pavlov famously demonstrated with dogs that learned to salivate at an unrelated external stimulus (Pavlov entering the room without food), fear can be learned and then stored in our unconscious.[10] An example might be a traumatic car accident. Years after the crash occurred, a victim may unexpectedly be paralyzed with fear at a cocktail party after simply hearing a familiar song in the background. The song just happens to be the very tune that was playing when the accident occurred. While the cocktail party itself presents no logical immediate danger, the victim can be overcome with dread.

These associations between brain and stimuli are called "memory triggers."[11] When a memory trigger is learned, it is stored in a region of the brain called the amygdala. When a person encounters the original stimulus, the brain unconsciously and automatically triggers the emotion tied to the stimulus. In the example of the car crash, the stimulus is the music and the automatic emotional reaction is fear.

This explains how people can be irrationally afraid of stimuli that to others appear completely innocuous. Memory triggers also explain how our fear responses are unconscious and out of our control. As Joseph Ledoux put it in a *New York Times* article on the subject, "We respond to danger, then only afterward realize danger is present."[12]

Not all memory triggers are bad. A hot stove remains just as dangerous every time you place your hand on it, so the mental reminder of the first time you touched one is quite helpful. But irrational memory triggers like the song in the car crash can be misleading and even dangerous. You don't want to repeat mistakes, but you also don't want to miss opportunities because of an automatic emotional response.

This poses an important question for your brand: What memory triggers does your organization have—and what is your reflexive response? When navigating The Wild, recognizing your own tendencies can be the difference between progress and paralysis.

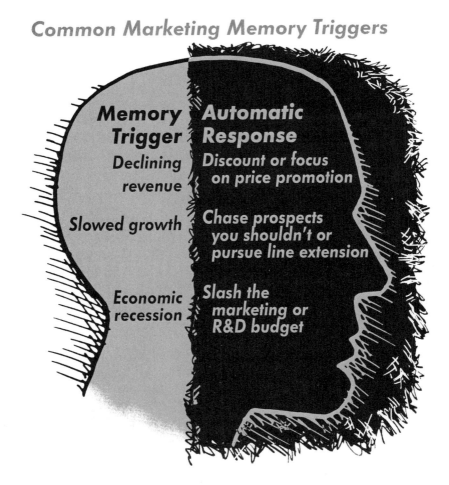

Figure 2.1 *Common Marketing Memory Triggers*

Why Fear Is Formed

It's one thing to understand the roots of fear, but parsing the reasons you are afraid is another matter. Many environmental conditions can cause fear, including overstimulation, cognitive incongruity, and response unavailability.[13] Or, in simpler terms, fear arises when you're overwhelmed, unprepared, or dealing with the unexpected. Unfamiliarity, proximity, and a lack of control can play a role as well.[14]

> ***Overwhelmed:*** What physiology calls overstimulation marketers call information overload. The amount of new information you are trying to process correlates with the amount of fear you feel. In other words, as information processing grows, fear rises. In The Wild, one of the first emotions you must deal with is a feeling of being overwhelmed. Economic instability, aggressive competitive moves, and disruptions in your industry can unload on you unfathomable amounts of unfamiliar data. Anticipating that information overload may cause you to react with fear is the first step toward entering Leach's top 10 in the 10–80–10 theory.
>
> ***Unprepared:*** Preparedness is also related to fear. When you are facing a difficult environment and don't know how to handle it, you are said to be dealing with response unavailability. One can see an example of this phenomenon in the 80 percent of survivors that Leach says respond to crisis with shock and numbness. Many stories have been documented in which someone survives a horrific accident only to die unnecessarily because he wasn't prepared to deal with the subsequent danger.
>
> A famous example is the 1985 Manchester airliner incident, in which a Boeing-737 suffered an engine fire while on the tarmac. While the people on board had plenty of time to exit the smoldering aircraft, many of the fifty-five people who died sat frozen in their seats until they succumbed to smoke inhalation.[15] In the end, it's not enough to survive The Wild; you must be prepared to navigate it.

Unexpected: Much of life and marketing can be boiled down to expectations, and when it comes to fear, the same holds true. People who do not adapt well to unexpected events often deal with cognitive incongruity. Cognitive incongruity is a state in which a person has difficulty reconciling with a specific event. For example, loss of a loved one or loss of a job can fall into this category. Fundamentally, it is a state in which a person simultaneously tries to hold two opposing views. Someone dealing with the loss of a loved one might say things like, "I can't believe she's gone," and may even find herself picking up the phone to call the lost loved one, only to remember she is not there.

For a marketer lost in the wilderness, cognitive incongruity usually manifests itself in denial. The Wild almost always creates an unexpected environment that is difficult (if not impossible) to predict and even harder to process in real time. If we know a danger is coming, we can begin to emotionally deal with the repercussions. But the extent to which an event is a surprise is the extent to which we react with fear. If you aren't facing the realities of your predicament, you've been scared into denial.

Unfamiliar: Surprisingly, danger and fear aren't always correlated. Humans are able to live with incredible amounts of danger if they are familiar enough with it, and the stats prove this. Almost three thousand people were shot in Chicago in 2015, yet terrorism is likely to be perceived by Chicagoans as representing a greater danger to their personal safety.[16] Nearly 88,000 alcohol-related deaths are recorded annually, yet comparatively rare shark attacks become burning topics across America.[17] The degree to which something is unfamiliar correlates with the degree to which we fear it.

The Wild, by definition, represents a departure from the status quo and is thus unfamiliar. While it is impossible to anticipate the endless unknowns The Wild has to offer, it is possible to begin familiarizing yourself with the unfamiliar, if not look forward to it, a concept and practice we will explore in depth in later chapters.

Proximity: Another driver of fear is proximity. Al Qaeda wasn't widely accepted as a problem until 9/11, and Ebola wasn't a top-of-mind concern until it showed up in an American hospital. The closer a danger is perceived to be, the more we fear it. The proximity principle can be especially deceptive in business, as potential dangers are easy to dismiss as affecting other industries and irrelevant in the short term. But disruptive innovation and the ability to speed up time to market have increased by such a degree that nearly every danger considered to be somewhere in the distant future could make it to your doorstep by morning. RadioShack, BlackBerry, and myriad other brands should have all seen their existential threats looming closer, yet all were slow or resistant to act.

Powerless: The final driver of fear is perceived control. It is well documented that it is nineteen times safer to fly than to drive, yet many of us still get a knot in our stomachs when we enter an airplane without having thought twice about the dangers of driving to the airport.[18] As Madhukar Trivedi, chair of the University of Texas-Southwestern's Mental Health Department, explained, "in a car, at least I know when to brake. In a plane, I have no control."[19]

As our real or perceived sense of control diminishes, our fear grows. The Wild can be especially debilitating in this regard, as it almost always destroys a management team's sense of control. Feeling helpless in the face of shifting technology or aggressive competition is normal. But beware a more dangerous error; worse than losing control is assuming you ever had it in the first place.

How Fear Happens

Ironically, being afraid can actually increase the likelihood that the feared thing will happen. As Christopher Bader, a Chapman sociology professor who studies fear, told the *New York Times*, "even if our fears are irra-tional, that can lead us to make choices that will actually cause the thing that we are avoiding."[20] Thus, fear of a specific part of town causes fewer people to live, work, or shop there, which in turn makes it a more dan-gerous part of town. In the financial world, a bank run only occurs when people begin pulling out their money, which causes mass hysteria, which causes even more people to pull out their money.

Fear causes fear causes fear. In other words, you should fear fear. In The Wild, you are often your greatest enemy, and your actions may con-tribute to the things you fear most coming to pass.

The long slide into the abyss of fear looks something like this: The Wild generates new (unexpected) and dangerously large amounts of information (overwhelming) into your immediate circumstance (prox-imity) that, according to Leach, 90 percent of people are not equipped (unprepared) to handle. New conditions are, by definition, different (unfamiliar). And different is scary. Fear causes an automatic and pre-programmed physiological response (fight-flight-freeze) that in turn can increase the risk of the feared thing happening.

I have watched countless companies follow the long slide to the point at which they actually have a hand in causing the very thing they are try-ing to avoid. The long slide can affect the simplest marketing decisions, like considering a new form of communications, as well as truly signifi-cant brand challenges that require the focus and alignment of large and often dysfunctional teams.

When you sense you are in the midst of the long slide, demystifying the role of fear and asserting control over it is the only way to avoid the abyss. But that is a course of action Kodak failed to pursue as it suffered from nearly every driver of fear. Kodak's initial decision to fight the rise of digital photography was followed by half-hearted measures to inte-grate the technology into its core film business.[21] Instead of investing in products that would eventually disrupt and replace its own lucrative but declining dominance in film, Kodak tried to use the technology to improve film quality.[22]

The Long Slide

Figure 2.2   *The Long Slide*

The company's growing sense of denial was best exemplified in its digital imaging R&D program. Instead of going all in on digital, Kodak implemented a program that was under constant pressure to both extend the life of film and find ways to integrate digital and film offerings.[23]

Kodak further evidenced its long slide into the abyss of fear via a revealing board decision in 1989. That was the year that CEO Colby Chandler stepped down, creating an opportunity for the outwardly successful but inwardly ailing company to chart a new course. But the board decided to pass on contender Phil Samper, an advocate of digital photography, in order to hire company veteran Kay R. Whitmore, who said he "would make sure Kodak stayed closer to its core businesses in film and photographic chemicals."[24] Looking back on Kodak's demise, one can see an institutional paralysis as CEO after CEO repeatedly gave lip service to digital photography while failing to follow through on every internal attempt.[25]

By 2001, Kodak's greatest fears began to be realized as film sales dropped and digital cameras were priced for the masses. Kodak recognized its vulnerable position and rushed a digital camera to market, using its extensive distribution network to take a market-leading position. But by 2007, competitors poured into the market, and Kodak was ranked number four in sales. That same year, the iPhone was introduced, featuring an embedded digital camera.

By 2010, the company had fully entered the abyss and began desperately pursuing other sources of income, including patent litigation. It all came to a sad and unnecessary end in 2012 when Kodak, a once-stalwart brand representing American ingenuity, creativity, and enterprise, filed for bankruptcy.[26] Thus ended more than one hundred years of film industry dominance.

Amazon Source to Sea

As the journey down the Amazon River drew on, Joe Kane's fear consumed his mind. His every thought was filled with dread of getting on the river, terror while navigating it, or brief hours of relief as the team camped for the night. Reflecting on his fear, Kane felt that he "might never escape the abyss, that it would never end."[27]

After Kane survived his harrowing climb above the river, he watched one of his fellow expeditionaries climb a river boulder and finally understood what he must have looked like clinging to a wall with sewing-machine legs not long before. In a moment of terror, Kane's companion stiffened like a stone. Kane observed that "His eyes were frozen. He looked paralyzed. I knew the feeling."[28]

The Amazon Source to Sea expedition would finally escape the endless jungle and complete its goal, but it's difficult to describe the ordeal as a success. The river nearly tore the expedition apart, literally and figuratively, and through its terror created irreconcilable differences between the expedition members.

In one of Kane's darker moments, he looked out over the great Amazon River, the source of his drowning fear and his only route home, and wrote, "Cold, hungry, and scared, I doubted whether I, or any of us, would survive the abyss."[29]

More than any natural danger, fear represents the first treacherous threat to navigating The Wild. While Joe Kane's expedition dealt with enormous rapids, food rationing, and interpersonal conflict, oppressive fear was the expedition's most insidious companion, creating internal factions that nearly led the expedition to self-destruction.

When you feel your natural fear response to The Wild welling up inside, remember that you're not alone. Every lost brand is afraid, and each must deal with its automatic and unconscious fear response. By understanding your brand's own memory triggers and decoding the long slide into the abyss, you can take an important step toward combatting fear's ill effects.

Don't despair. Yes, fear can wreak havoc. But if you're scared, you're alive.

Survival Tips for Practical Application

Focus on decoding and demystifying fear as you grapple with the first internal dynamic that brands deal with when lost in the wilderness.

Keep in Mind

- Paralyzing fear is the first reaction when brands are lost in the wilderness.
- Lost brands are statistically more likely to fear risk, resist change, and be reluctant to invest.
- Your automatic and unconscious biological response to fear is rigged to make you irrational and erratic.

Survival Tips

To navigate The Wild:

- Diagnose your organization's memory triggers and automatic responses.
- Beware the conditions that contribute to fear: information overload, lack of preparation, the unexpected, the unfamiliar, proximity, and lack of control.
- Decode the long slide, the natural process that can lead to self-fulfilling fear.

Notes

1. Joe Kane, *Running the Amazon* (New York: Vintage Books, 1990), 164.
2. Kane, *Running the Amazon*, 165–166.
3. Lisa Fritscher, "The Psychology of Fear: Understanding the Dynamics of the Fear Response," *Verywell.com*, March 7, 2016, https://www.verywell.com/the-psychology-of-fear-2671696.
4. Alex Carl, "What Kodak Can Teach Us about Avoiding Failure," Device Magic (blog), February 6, 2015, http://www.devicemagic.com/blog/kodak-moment.
5. Kamal Munir, "The Demise of Kodak: Five Reasons," *The Wall Street Journal*, February 26, 2012, http://blogs.wsj.com/source/2012/02/26/the-demise-of-kodak-five-reasons/.
6. Chunka Mui, "How Kodak Failed," *Forbes*, January 19, 2012, http://www.forbes.com/sites/chunkamui/2012/01/18/how-kodak-failed/#6405 1b88bd6a.
7. Mui, "How Kodak Failed."
8. Kane, *Running the Amazon*, 172.
9. Kane, *Running the Amazon*, 173.
10. Joseph Ledoux, "Searching the Brain for the Roots of Fear," *The New York Times*, January 22, 2012, http://opinionator.blogs.nytimes.com/2012/01/22/anatomy-of-fear/?_r=0.
11. Ledoux, "Searching the Brain for the Roots of Fear."

12. Ledoux, "Searching the Brain for the Roots of Fear."

13. Carissa Kelvens, *Fear and Anxiety* (Northridge: California State University), 1997, accessed August 7, 2016, http://www.csun.edu/~vcpsy00h/students/fear.htm.

14. Olga Khazan, "The Psychology of Irrational Fear: Why We're More Afraid of Sharks than Car Accidents, and of Ebola than Flu," *The Atlantic*, October 31, 2014, http://www.theatlantic.com/health/archive/2014/10/the-psychology-of-irrational-fear/382080/.

15. John Leach, "Survival Psychology: The Won't to Live," *The Psychologist.com*, January 2011, https://thepsychologist.bps.org.uk/volume-24/edition-1/survival-psychology-wont-live.

16. Samuel Lieberman, "The 2016 Gun-Violence Statistics Out of Chicago Are Horrific," *New York Magazine*, January 12, 2016, http://nymag.com/daily/intelligencer/2016/01/2016-chicago-gun-violence-stats-are-horrific.html.

17. "Alcohol Facts and Statistics," National Institute on Alcohol Abuse and Alcoholism, June 2016, https://www.niaaa.nih.gov/alcohol-health/overview-alcohol-consumption/alcohol-facts-and-statistics.

18. "How Safe Is Commercial Flight?" *Axieties.com*, accessed September 3, 2016, http://anxieties.com/flying-howsafe.php#.V1G_uJMrL_R.

19. Khazan, "The Psychology of Irrational Fear."

20. Khazan, "The Psychology of Irrational Fear."

21. Munir, "The Demise of Kodak: Five Reasons."

22. Mui, "How Kodak Failed."

23. Munir, "The Demise of Kodak: Five Reasons."

24. John Holusha, "Click: Up, Down and Out at Kodak," *The New York Times*, December 9, 1989, http://www.nytimes.com/1989/12/09/business/click-up-down-and-out-at-kodak.html.

25. Mui, "How Kodak Failed."

26. Carl, "What Kodak Can Teach Us about Avoiding Failure."

27. Kane, *Running the Amazon*, 181.

28. Kane, *Running the Amazon*, 168.

29. Kane, *Running the Amazon*, 187.

CHAPTER 3

Adrift

After sitting for five weeks waiting for the ice to open, Stefansson became impatient. He was a leader who thrived on activity, and the delay hardly suited him . . . dreading the prospect of inaction, Stefansson set out on a personal expedition. On September 19, he abruptly announced that he was going to hunt for caribou . . . Stefansson loaded two sledges with food and ammunition and, after posing for photographs, set out with four others for Point Barrow.[1]

—Dennis N. T. Perkins, *Leading at the Edge*

Vilhjalmur Stefansson wasn't expecting this: after months of preparation, an official mandate from the Canadian government, and a very public send-off, the anthropologist and explorer was trapped on his ship. The twenty-four-foot wooden fishing vessel named *Karluk* was packed between the crushing weight of endless ice, hundreds of miles from its destination.

None of the thirty-two members of the expedition expressed any concern during the first few weeks on the ice, thinking that it would eventually dissipate. But by the fifth week, Stefansson worried that the ship might be destroyed—or, worse, would drift for years locked in an endless winter.

Stefansson had set out on June 17, 1913, with a team of scientists, geologists, and locals to lead the Canadian Arctic Expedition and help Canada lay claim to the Arctic islands.[2] He also hoped to discover a continent somewhere beneath the ice north of Alaska.

But only two months into the journey, the expedition's ill-equipped fishing ship was caught between quickly forming ice fields just over two hundred miles north of Alaska.

As the long wait on the ice drew on, Stefansson's patience grew thin. Near the end of September, he announced to the ship's captain that he was going to take two sledges, four men, hefty supplies, and the expedition's prized dogs on a ten-day caribou hunt.

Only two days into the hunt, disaster struck. The ice fields broke apart, separating Stefansson and his four companions from the crew left behind on the ship. The remaining crew members stood helpless on the ice as they drifted far beyond reach. Their subsequent desperate struggle to survive would be forever remembered as "The *Karluk* Disaster."[3]

Stefansson's exercise in impatience and distraction is an example of an all-too-common phenomenon in marketing. When economic changes, aggressive competition, or disruption cause brands to lose their way, they will first suffer paralyzing fear then watch as their ability to focus falters.

Focus is the preeminent skill of all great marketers. It is the foundation of differentiation and the most important discipline in branding. Focus is also the hardest thing to accomplish and the easiest thing to lose. Our research reveals that companies struggling with growth are five times more likely to have lost their focus than companies enjoying healthy growth.

As those who have experienced a threatening situation can attest, when the body initiates the fight-flight-freeze response, the most basic environmental information is difficult to process and observe, let alone the most important information.

As the body floods itself with three key hormones in response to fear, it receives a boost of energy, increases the heart rate, and begins the process of bronchial dilation that enables the lungs to take in more oxygen.[4] In the midst of this rush of activity, the pupils dilate, which narrows the field of vision and limits your ability to observe and process peripheral information. In other words, when you're afraid, your body screams for action while your mind experiences tunnel vision. Despite sounding similar to focus, it is actually the opposite.

Focus requires an awareness of all of the surrounding environmental information, which is then excluded in favor of a specific point of concentration. Tunnel vision, by contrast, is the lack of awareness of surrounding information and the inability to even observe it. That means that not only do people in difficult situations lack the information they need to make smart decisions, they are effectively blind to it.

I call this dangerous mix of tunnel vision and an intense need for action the "drift dilemma." The drift dilemma hit Stefansson hard as he struggled with the dual threat of an internal drive for action and no clear way to accomplish his exploratory goals while trapped on the ice. At the time, the hunting excursion would scratch Stefansson's itch for action, which he justified by promising to supply food for the expedition. But in retrospect, it was a dangerous diversion that led to disaster.

In marketing, the drift dilemma is exemplified by those brands that make decisions that seem obviously misguided in retrospect but are not recognized by decision makers as poor options in the moment.

Microsoft's 2013 Xbox One video game console launch now infamously fits that category. The launch was meant to reposition Microsoft's game console as a comprehensive entertainment platform, but instead it turned into a case study on how a bold vision isn't a substitute for disciplined focus. Microsoft intended for the new Xbox One to be used more like a unified family entertainment device, incorporating online streaming, Blu-ray, DVD, and social media connectivity. Most importantly, the Xbox One was built to take full advantage of Microsoft's powerful new video motion-sensing device, the Kinect, enabling users to interact with the device without a controller.

The company's vision was brave, but its execution represented a failure of focus. Because the launch of a new console traditionally only occurs every three to five years, Microsoft felt pressured to force-fit its vision into the console by requiring that it come bundled with the Kinect device and be connected to the Internet at all times in order to function.

This resulted in a significant price point for the console and considerable concern in the press about an always-connected video device in America's living rooms.

Bolder still, Microsoft intended to embrace the growing trend toward digital video game retail and prevent revenue loss to the lively used game market by requiring a digital code for every offline game purchase.

For all of Microsoft's well-intentioned vision, the result would be one of the biggest public relations fiascos in video game history and a case study in drift dilemma. Instead of introducing a visionary product built on the highly successful Xbox 360, Microsoft lost sight of its core customer and debuted an overpriced, underpowered console with new, restrictive technology that would effectively kill the robust used game market dominated by retail giant Game Stop.

Gamers revolted, the video game press screamed, and Sony pounced on the opportunity by debuting its new PlayStation 4 console at a lower price and publicly committing to never interfere with the used game market. The results of the public relations implosion were felt immediately and reverberated over the following years. Sony's PlayStation 4 nearly doubled Microsoft's Xbox One sales.[5] Microsoft neglected its core audience, hardcore gamers, and learned a hard lesson in focus.

Attack on Attention

Focus is just as much about seeing clearly as it is about consistently maintaining attention, and as research has proven, attention is a finite resource under incessant attack.

A University of California, Irvine, study showed that modern professionals have to switch tasks up to four hundred times a day.[6] While most of us intuitively understand the importance of attention, few understand that the human brain has limited neural resources that can actually run out. Winifred Gallagher, author of *Rapt*, estimates that the normal human brain can only process 173 billion bits of information over a lifetime.[7] To help wrap our minds around this lifetime limit, Mihaly Csikszentmihalyi, author of *Good Business: Leadership, Flow, and the Making of Meaning*, explains that we use about forty bits of brain power to understand what another person is saying to us.[8] Start adding up all of the bits our brain requires to read our morning emails, get the kids to school, drive to work, drink our coffee, and catch up on the day's headlines, and you quickly see how easy it is to reach your daily brain bit limit.

Continual shifts in attention actually deplete daily resources and work against our limited lifetime processing capacity.[9] Distraction doesn't only tempt us to lose focus, it actually depletes vital mental resources. The reason it's hard to get over the three o'clock hump or make decisions at the end of the day is because we are literally running out of daily brain bits. As Verena von Pfetten put it in a *New York Times* article about exhausting attention, "The term 'brain dead' suddenly takes on a whole new meaning."[10]

Mental fatigue is real. The onslaught of information The Wild throws at you isn't just emotionally overwhelming, it literally overwhelms your brain and makes focus a monumental task. The moment you desperately need mental resources may be just the time your limit is reached. Worse, you may further deplete your own neural resources by actually entertaining distractions.

A Harvard study found that multitasking releases dopamine into the brain, the same neurotransmitter associated with pleasure and addiction.[11] Multitasking activities can include everything from switching attention throughout the day to checking email. With each activity, the brain receives a small dose of dopamine that reinforces the action.

Rasmus Hougaard, coauthor of *One Second Ahead: Enhance Your Performance at Work with Mindfulness*, explains that "Most of us have action addiction; it's that dopamine craving. . . . Shifting back and forth between tasks often feels exciting, even though it's physically draining and stressful."

The problem with action is that it always feels good, even when it isn't. Just as Stefansson's impatience and penchant for action led to unnecessary risk and eventual ruin for the crew of the *Karluk*, action for action's sake in marketing can be wasteful and disastrous.

Starbucks's well-documented decline in 2006 and 2007, followed by the iconic turnaround efforts of CEO Howard Schultz, can be traced to a bad case of action addiction. After Schultz stepped down from the helm in 2000,[12] Starbucks's leadership team pursued an aggressive growth strategy. Over the following seven years, it added nearly ten thousand stores,[13] expanded its retail music program, and dove into new product offerings like breakfast sandwiches.

Upon returning in 2008, Schultz refocused the company on "the authenticity of the coffee experience" and immediately cut unfocused activity by slowing the rate of growth, closing more than six hundred stores, reinventing the breakfast sandwich menu, and overhauling the entertainment division.[14]

Commenting on what led to Starbucks's action addiction and subsequent decline, Schultz wrote that there wasn't a precise moment or obvious misstep one could point to, but that "the damage was slow and quiet, incremental, like a single loose thread that unravels a sweater inch by inch."[15] Growth and activity, while good, are not ends in themselves and, when blindly pursued, can lead to a loss of focus. Don't mistake activity for progress. Just because you're moving doesn't mean you're going in the right direction.

Focus Is Choice with Purpose

The brain's ongoing struggle against endless distractions underscores the fundamental nature of focus; at its core, focus is choice. Ultimately, your brand can represent anything. It is the exercise of choice that makes your brand represent something. The more "anythings" you choose not to be, the more powerful your "something" can be.

Thrashing what she insists is the myth of multitasking, Winifred Gallagher breaks down focus to its essence, explaining, "You cannot do two things at once. The mechanism of attention is selection: it's either this or it's that."[16]

Apple became a titan of industry and technology because it *isn't* so many things. It *isn't* about freedom, offering consumers choices, or providing an endless array of features. Apple *is* about curating and simplifying a user experience.

Southwest Airlines *isn't* about in-flight options, a high-end experience, or offering flights everywhere in the world. Southwest *is* about low-cost transportation with heart.

But making a choice isn't enough. In order to find focus, one must know how to make the *right* choice. And to make the right choice, you need purpose.

While Howard Schultz was forced to address costs and overhead issues at Starbucks, it wasn't all about dollars. In an *Inc.* magazine interview about the turnaround, Schultz said, "The customer today is very well informed. In addition to price and convenience, there's something else they are influenced by, and that's what the company stands for."

Stefansson faced a crisis of purpose when trapped on the ice more than a century ago. While the stated purpose of the expedition was to explore the Arctic, Stefansson was a well-known self-promoter famous for dubbing the inhospitable north the "Friendly Arctic."[17] Throughout his career, he was more interested in promoting his exploits than in actually completing them.[18] With a purpose so untethered to the realities of arctic exploration, becoming distracted with a hunting excursion just weeks into the expedition's first hardship isn't surprising, but it was dangerous.

Contrast Stefansson with Google, which states that its purpose is to "organize the world's information and make it universally accessible and useful."[19] With such a well-defined purpose that is both broad enough to encompass nearly anything and narrow enough to align thousands of employees, Google's leadership has the foundation it needs to make focused choices.

As all busy professionals can attest, knowing that focus is important is very different from actually exercising the discipline of focus. The good news is that research from Robert Desimone, a neuroscientist at MIT, points to the fact that our ability to focus is something that can actually be strengthened like a muscle.

Dr. Desimone's research uses the visual system in humans and monkeys to study the brain's ability to focus on certain tasks while filtering out irrelevant information.[20] Desimone uses flashes of light to try to grab the attention of his subjects, then studies the impact on different regions in the brain. Through his research, Desimone discovered that external stimuli that enter the brain (distractions in the form of light) can actually be overridden by the prefrontal cortex in a process he calls "biased competition."[21] The brain uses neurons that fire in unison, which Desimone describes "like a chorus rising above the noise," to direct the brain to focus on the desired object of attention.[22] In short, in the battle for your attention, your brain wins by making your neurons work together to gang up on distraction. The more you force your neurons to work together, the stronger your gang becomes.

Psychologists who study attention call the ability to control behavior "executive function," which represents a suite of cognitive skills that inform our ability to focus.[23] Executive function can be thought of as something akin to Desimone's biased competition and requires the coordination and harmony of multiple cognitive skills to consistently attain focus. For the complicated, multifaceted organizations that modern brands embody today, the "suite of cognitive skills" is a multilayered web of departments, leadership, culture, and purpose that must be aligned and navigated to find and retain focus. When this suite of cognitive skills breaks down, attention suffers.

Enemies of Focus

As action addiction and Desimone's "biased competition" demonstrate, at any given moment, you are either reinforcing your addiction to distraction or improving your ability to focus. For brands—and the marketers who shepherd them—there is no in between. But before you can consistently choose to exercise your "focus muscle," you must understand the enemies working against it: *success*, *misdiagnosis*, *complacency*, and *placation*. It just so happens that retail giant Circuit City struggled with them all during its decade-long descent into irrelevance.

Success: Circuit City used to be one of the largest and most successful electronics retailers in the world. It built its own category and, in its heyday, owned more than 1,500 locations, employed more than 46,000 people, and enjoyed annual revenue as high as $12 billion. But as new competitors entered the market and consumer behavior shifted, Circuit City remained static.

Circuit City's market share began to slide when Best Buy responded to changing consumer behavior by stocking low-margin inventory like video games and CDs and moving away from the traditional commission-based sales force.[24] Circuit City's resistance and mismanagement of both issues would contribute to its decline, but a larger problem loomed for the retailer: it continued to see strong sales despite its lack of innovation.

As competitors outmaneuvered the retail giant, strong sales hid the underlying problems. Alan Wurtzel, son of Circuit City's founder and CEO of the company for thirteen years, said that the retailer's loss of focus "wasn't obvious in sales and earnings, but the rot had set in." In the midst of the industrywide sea change, 2000 would be Circuit City's most successful year, but the seeds of ruin were already sown.[25]

Misdiagnosis: Steve McKee, branding expert and author of *When Growth Stalls*, points out that companies tend to lose focus in one of two ways: either the market shifts around them or they lose focus internally.[26] Correct diagnosis of the situation is the difference between course correction and continued decline.

Stefansson faced both impediments to focus on his Arctic expedition, first battling the crush of the unexpected summer ice field then losing focus internally and pursuing a foolish distraction. He managed to correctly diagnose the challenge of the ice fields, as his concern about a long wait on the drifting ice would prove true. But his lack of self-awareness would lead to his personal loss of focus and the ill-conceived hunting trip.

Circuit City, on the other hand, failed to diagnose both its internal and external problems as it experienced a shifting marketplace while clinging to an outdated business model. Circuit City's focus first came under attack from a number of copycats like Best Buy and Costco that diluted the electronic retail market in the 1980s and 1990s. But Circuit City's greatest threat came when consumer behavior began to shift and the management team didn't respond. Misstep after misstep betrayed their misdiagnosis of the situation, including the decision to stop selling appliances and neglecting an outdated web presence as Amazon began its ascent.[27] Wurtzel believes Circuit City's puzzling misdiagnosis was due to tunnel vision, explaining, "We thought we were smarter than anybody."[28]

Complacency: Perhaps the most insidious threat to focus, complacency is a toxic mix of apathy and overconfidence that can destroy the mightiest brand's focus. Although Circuit City's leadership was aware of cause for concern, Alan Wurtzel believes management didn't have a sense of urgency, saying, "there was an arrogance."[29]

The shortest path to distraction is through complacency, and by the mid-1990s and 2000s, Circuit City made a number of unfocused moves that left experts scratching their heads. The company acquired a Canadian electronics chain, invested in a new DVD technology, and built up and sold the retail car brand CarMax, which divided the attention of senior management and even pulled several members of the C-suite away during the sale.[30]

Looking back on the loss of focus, Wurtzel cautioned that complacency and a lack of humility are two sides of the same coin, warning that "the time you get in trouble is when you think you know the answers."[31]

Placation: Stefansson, an explorer and self-promoter during the twentieth century's golden age of exploration, was a well-known busybody with a penchant for constant action. His decision to leave his vulnerable, icebound expedition for a ten-day hunt wasn't just foolish, it was an exercise in self-mollification. In that moment, Stefansson chose to indulge his own need for activity instead of protecting the needs of the thirty-one other members of his expedition.

In a similar way, as Circuit City's sales declined to a point of concern and then crisis in the years leading up to 2007, the ailing retailer began to make decisions aimed more at placating restless shareholders than serving disaffected customers.

In a play to please Wall Street, the electronics retailer fired thousands of its top-performing salespeople, slashed commissions, and pursued an expand-at-all-costs strategy that led to the selection of subpar store locations. While it succeeded in cutting costs and expanding quickly, it did so by sacrificing customer service.

Experts also point to a controversial stock buyback program during Circuit City's long sales decline between 2003 and 2007 that left it penniless when it faced a cash crunch during the Great Recession.[32] Remarking on Circuit City's sad tale, Doug Bosse, professor of strategy at the University of Richmond, said, "It's not a story where they did one thing really badly. . . . It's a story of hundreds and hundreds of smaller decisions that added up to be destructive."[33]

The *Karluk* Disaster

After watching the remaining twenty-seven crew members of the *Karluk* drift away, Stefansson and his four companions continued their journey of exploration and geologic survey. They would disappear from civilization for a full five years before suddenly reappearing in 1918, never assuming responsibility for the fate of the remaining expedition members.

The ship's captain, Robert Barlett, did his best to stand in the leadership void, but the crushing ice and cold desperation would lead to catastrophe for much of the crew. After Stefansson's disappearance, the *Karluk* continued to drift for another four months until the ice finally punctured the hull of the ship and forced the crew onto the frozen surface.

Barlett insisted that the stranded expedition continue to winter on the floating ice for fear of traveling through the polar darkness. But several crew members deserted their companions when they found running water on an excursion to an island. Their skeletons would later be found by a subsequent expedition.

When winter finally passed, Barlett led the desperate group of inexperienced travelers 150 miles across the ice to land. There, he and a single companion embarked on a seven-hundred-mile journey south to find help. His perilous trek paid off when the Canadian ship *King and Winge* rescued the survivors nearly a year later, in September 1914. In the meantime, eleven of the original expedition members died of exposure and starvation.

Looking back at blunders like Stefansson's folly and Circuit City's crash, it is easy to point out obvious missteps and respond with incredulity. But in the moment, no leader intentionally embraces distractions. They're simply blind to them.

It is through the predictable physiological response to fear that we can begin to see drift dilemma for what it is: a dangerous combination of a lack of perspective and a drive for focus-destroying action for action's sake. By remaining aware of the dangers of action addiction and pursuit of distraction, you can begin to assess your situation and vigilantly avoid the foes of focus.

Just as Barlett rallied the expedition and saved fourteen lives, you too can reclaim focus. If you don't, the next step in the descent into savagery will turn you, and your brand, wild.

Survival Tips for Practical Application

Examine your predisposition toward distraction as you wrestle with the second internal dynamic that brands face when lost in the wilderness.

Keep in Mind

- A breakdown in focus is a brand's second reaction to The Wild.
- Companies struggling with growth are five times more likely to have lost their focus than companies enjoying healthy growth.
- In extreme situations, your body simultaneously experiences tunnel vision and an intense need for action, a toxic mix known as drift dilemma.

Survival Tips

To navigate The Wild:

- Diagnose the assault on your limited supply of attention.
- Beware the enemies of focus: *success*, *misdiagnosis*, *complacency*, and *placation*.
- Remember that focus is choice with purpose and can be learned and strengthened.

Notes

1. Dennis N. T. Perkins, *Leading at the Edge: Leadership Lessons from the Extraordinary Saga of Shackleton's Antarctic Expedition* (New York: Amacom, 2000), 21–22.
2. Jenny Higgins, "The Karluk Disaster," *Newfoundland & Labrador Heritage*, 2008, accessed August 12, 2016, http://www.heritage.nf.ca/articles/exploration/karluk-disaster.php.
3. Higgins, "The Karluk Disaster."
4. Brad Fitzpatrick, "Your Brain on Survival: Here's What Happens When the Body Shifts into Survival Mode, and How You Can Stay in Control," *Outdoor Life*, 223, no. 3 (April 2016): 47.

5. Charles Poladian, "PS4 vs. Xbox One: Close to 40 Million PlayStation 4 Consoles Have Been Sold Since 2013 Launch," *International Business Times*, April 28, 2016, http://www.ibtimes.com/ps4-vs-xbox-one-close-40-million-playstation-4-consoles-have-been-sold-2013-launch-2361021.

6. Gloria Mark, Shamsi T. Iqbal, Mary Czerwinski, Paul Johns, and Akane Sano, "Neurotics Can't Focus: An in Situ Study of Online Multitasking in the Workplace," accessed July 10, 2016, http://www.ics.uci.edu/~gmark/Home_page/Research_files/CHI%2016%20Multitasking%20and%20Focus.pdf.

7. John Tierney, "Ear Plugs to Lasers: The Science of Concentration," *The New York Times*, May 4, 2016, http://www.nytimes.com/2009/05/05/science/05tier.html?_r=1.

8. Mihaly Csikszentmihalyi, *Good Business: Leadership, Flow, and the Making of Meaning* (New York: Penguin Books, 2004).

9. Verena von Pfetten, "Read This Story without Distraction (Can You?)," *The New York Times*, April 29, 2016, http://www.nytimes.com/2016/05/01/fashion/monotasking-drop-everything-and-read-this-story.html.

10. Pfetten, "Read This Story without Distraction (Can You?)."

11. Stephanie Vozza, "The Science behind Daydreaming and How You Can Retrain Your Brain to Focus," *Fast Company*, February 3, 2016, http://www.fastcompany.com/3056146/work-smart/the-science-behind-day-dreaming-and-how-you-can-retrain-your-brain-to-focus.

12. NBCUniversal, "Starbucks Chairman Schultz Returning as CEO," *NBCNews.com*, January 8, 2008, http://www.nbcnews.com/id/22544023/ns/business-us_business/t/starbucks-chairman-schultz-returning-ceo/#.V91st9MrKgQ.

13. Aimee Groth, "19 Amazing Ways CEO Howard Schultz Saved Starbucks," *Business Insider*, June 19, 2011, http://www.businessinsider.com/howard-schultz-turned-starbucks-around-2011–6?op=1.

14. Groth, "19 Amazing Ways CEO Howard Schultz Saved Starbucks."

15. Howard Schultz and Joanne Gordon, "Introduction," in *Onward: How Starbucks Fought for Its Life without Losing Its Soul* (New York: Rodale, 2011), xiv.

16. Tierney, "Ear Plugs to Lasers."

17. William J. Buxton, ed., *Harold Innis and the North: Appraisals and Contestations* (Montreal & Kingston: McGill-Queen's University Press, 2013), 199.

18. Perkins, *Leading at the Edge*, 21.

19. Google, "Company Overview," Google Company, accessed September 1, 2016, https://www.google.com/about/company/.
20. Robert Desimone, Mcgovern.mit.edu, June 22, 2016, https://mcgovern.mit.edu/principal-investigators/robert-desimone.
21. Tierney, "Ear Plugs to Lasers: The Science of Concentration."
22. "Research: Attending to Important Matters," Desimone Laboratory McGovern Institute, accessed August 9, 2016, http://desimonelab.org/research/.
23. Jonah Lehrer, "Focusing on Focus," *Wired.com*, September 6, 2011, http://www.wired.com/2011/09/focusing-on-focus/.
24. Jessie Romero, "Economic History: The Rise and Fall of Circuit City," 2013, accessed July 25, 2016, https://www.richmondfed.org/~/media/richmondfed org/publications/research/econ_focus/2013/q3/pdf/economic_history.pdf.
25. Rachel Feintzeig, "Lessons from the Death of Circuit City," *The Wall Street Journal*, October 25, 2012, http://blogs.wsj.com/bankruptcy/2012/10/25/lessons-from-the-death-of-circuit-city/.
26. Steve McKee, *When Growth Stalls: How It Happens, Why You're Stuck, and What to Do about It* (San Francisco: Jossey-Bass, 2009), 58.
27. Anita Hamilton, "Why Circuit City Busted, While Best Buy Boomed," *Time*, November 11, 2008, http://content.time.com/time/business/article/0,8599,1858079,00.html.
28. Romero, "Economic History," 32.
29. Feintzeig, "Lessons from the Death of Circuit City."
30. Romero, "Economic History."
31. Romero, "Economic History," 32.
32. Romero, "Economic History."
33. Romero, "Economic History," 33.

CHAPTER 4

Wild

"Is it normal to fly so close?" one boy asked another.

"I don't think so," his companion replied.

Several passengers started to pray. . . . There was a roar of the engines and the plane vibrated as the Fairchild tried to climb again; it rose a little but then there came the deafening crash as the right wing hit the side of the mountain. Immediately, it broke off, somersaulted over the fuselage, and cut off the tail. Out into the icy air fell the steward, the navigator . . . followed by three of the boys still strapped to their seats.

—Piers Paul Read, *Alive*

The fuselage glided down the snowy mountaintop like a mangled model airplane landing on a pillow. The freak landing preserved lives, but the speed of the crash caused the metal and plastic seats to break from their mounts and slam against the front luggage compartment, crushing passengers caught in between.

A short silence filled the cabin, followed by a growing chorus of screams as the survivors took in their surroundings. Blood and terror mingled with the freezing mountain air. It was a scene of complete chaos and despair.

On October 12, 1972, an airplane filled with forty-five passengers, most members of a Uruguayan rugby team traveling to a match in Chile, crashed into an isolated region of the Andes Mountains. Following the impact, a handful of survivors began trying to help their fellow passengers. As they attempted to navigate the wreckage and pull people to safety, the full weight of the situation became apparent.

The front of the airplane had crumpled like a tin can, trapping the only surviving pilot between the cockpit door and the instrument panel that was now sunk into his chest. A woman screamed for help as her legs lay flattened under the wreckage. Many of the young men suffered broken arms, broken legs, major lacerations, metal lodged in their bodies, and muscles ripped from bone.

Most of those with only superficial wounds sat stunned, unable to move. The few who tried to help were hindered by several irrational passengers, like Carlos Valeta, who made the situation worse.

Shortly after exiting the wreckage, Valeta began to walk mindlessly away into the distance. As he wandered ever deeper into the thigh-high snow, his companions yelled for him to return. But their calls were met with silence, and he stumbled farther away until finally he slumped into the snow, disappearing from view.

Another young man helped the survivors despite suffering from amnesia. Although he was in fine physical condition, he didn't know who he was or why he was helping. Yet another survivor repeatedly attempted to hike down the mountain.

As daylight turned to dusk, the survivors dragged the wounded into the tiny fuselage and built a makeshift wall out of luggage and airplane seats to try to block the bitter cold from entering the gaping hole in the tail. Many of the young men began ravenously consuming the meager amount of food and wine that survived the crash, believing rescue would arrive in the morning.[1]

Two months later, they were still waiting.

Much like the unfortunate survivors of the Andes airplane crash, many brands lost in the wilderness commit a series of panicked, desperate actions that lack clear purpose. As a brand struggles with overpowering fear and loses its focus, it may pursue misguided activity in fits and starts. This sporadic activity can be a result of not knowing what else to do or (more often) is in pursuit of a silver-bullet solution. Wrestling with insecurity, brands will look for a quick and easy answer. As each silver bullet proves to be a dud, they move to the next one, misfire again, and repeat.

In short, The Wild turns brands wild. Our research tells us that struggling companies are four times more likely than healthy companies to say that their marketing is inconsistent.[2] This inconsistency is the third internal dynamic companies face after losing their way in the wilderness and is the natural result of fear and drift. A brand's erratic behavior is not only unhelpful, it will actually harm the company's efforts to rekindle growth. As with the Andes survivors, it may also be a sign that the end is near.

Wild behavior represents a special danger for lost brands. Inconsistency undermines many of the fundamental requirements of resilience. Shortsightedness encourages opportunistic behavior, undercuts strategy, and can actually increase desperation as tactic after tactic fails. As failure grows more common, the team will either slump into some form of learned helplessness or turn on one another, marking the last gasps of a descending brand.

To understand why brands and the people who lead them can succumb to such irrational behavior, it is helpful to look at one of the last physiological responses to fear. As the body endures a rush of hormones, pupil dilation, and increased blood circulation, the limbic system takes control of the brain.[3]

The limbic system is sometimes called the "feeling and reacting brain,"[4] as it controls our emotions, drives, instincts, and moods. As it takes over, it pushes aside the frontal lobe, which can be thought of as our "thinking brain."[5] With the limbic system in control, our thoughts and actions become more reflexive and less logical. Or, to put it simply, as pressure mounts, people get stupid.

A similar phenomenon has been well documented in underwater cave diving, where very real pressure has astounding effects on the mind and body. Still a relatively young sport, cave diving draws many novice and open-water scuba divers who don't understand the unique dangers of pressure. In utter darkness deep below the earth's surface, reports of divers experiencing extreme vertigo and losing their sense of up and down are common. Many divers have even died within feet of a cave entrance with plenty of air still in their tanks.[6]

The most common danger of pressure is called Raptures of the Deep. The phenomenon, also known as nitrogen narcosis, causes an effect similar to that of drinking a martini for every thirty feet of depth. The more pressure a diver experiences, the more confused and illogical she becomes.[7] The analogy is uncomfortably fitting in business. As a company deals with mounting pressure, its actions often resemble those of a drowning drunk more than those of a disciplined professional.

One of the challenges with companies driven by limbic-system thinking is that logic and reason rarely persuade them. With every opportunistic, irrational action, brands suffering from the third internal dynamic fall closer to a fate I call the " 'F' death spiral."

Dr. John Leach, professor at Lancaster University, mapped out the normal sequence of events involved in an extreme situation, including pre-impact, impact, recovery, rescue, and post-trauma.[8] During an extreme situation, people will experience the fight-flight-freeze reaction most acutely during the impact and recovery phases.

After an initial shock, many survivors who are experiencing the fight-flight-freeze response will eventually exit the impact and recovery phase and recapture the use of their frontal lobe, enabling them to calm down and think rationally during the rescue and post-trauma phases. This is an important step toward removing limbic system control and regaining logical thinking. The great danger for brands is to avoid dealing with the inconsistent behaviors that occur during their fight-flight-freeze response and get stuck bouncing between the three "F's" like a ball in a pinball machine. The result is something resembling brand "death."

This is the "F" death spiral. It is entirely avoidable and has more to do with mindset than with resources and capabilities. The propensity to

Leach's Sequence Map

Figure 4.1 *Leach's Map Sequence*

F Death Spiral

Figure 4.2 *F Death Spiral*

get stuck in an avoidable "F" death spiral is underscored by an example Leach points to in his research.

Two passengers and a pilot flying over the Sierra Nevada crashed in 1994. After the impact, the pilot suffered an extreme ankle sprain and injured ribs,[9] one of the passengers experienced some bruising, and the other was trapped inside the small aircraft but okay. Given their remote location, the pilot decided to attempt to hike through the mountains to find aid. The pilot hiked nearly forty miles and subsisted solely on snow and insects. After nine days, the pilot was able to find a road and ask the driver of a passing car for help. Within hours, the pilot led a rescue craft to the crash site, where they found both passengers dead, despite having suffered only limited injuries and having plenty of water and shelter.[10]

The difference between the injured pilot who struggled through a heroic nine-day journey and the relatively safe passengers who died at the crash site is the ability to break the "F" death spiral. The key to avoiding death-by-inconsistency is knowing how you will react when The Wild strikes.

Three common psychological behaviors manifest themselves when companies find themselves under pressure: hypoactivity/cognitive paralysis, stereotypical behavior/perseveration, and hyperactivity. You may not have control over these behaviors at the onset of a challenge, but understanding and overcoming them may mark the difference between falling into the "F" death spiral and breaking the cycle of inconsistency to find renewed growth.

Wild Brands Move Like Molasses

The first type of inconsistent behavior is hypoactivity and its kissing cousin, cognitive paralysis. Where hypoactivity is marked by a pronounced slowing in thought, speech, and movement,[11] cognitive paralysis is a state of complete inaction.

The survivors of the Andes airplane crash suffered from these behaviors in a variety of ways, even long after the immediate stress of the crash had passed. Roy Harley and Bobby Francois, young, strong, and capable rugby players, both survived the crash relatively unscathed. But as the survivors began to cope with the situation and dole out daily responsibilities, Harley and Francois would simply sit in the sun, unable to work. The group attributed Francois's stunned state to prolonged shock from the crash, whereas several personal losses for Harley left him without a sense of hope or purpose.[12] In both circumstances, the survivor's mental state trumped his physical capabilities.

Borders, a pioneer in the megabookstore category, suffered a similar fate as it faced its own wilderness experience. In a series of challenges that piled upon one another, the chain faced the digitization of music in the 1990s, followed by the rise of online retail and e-readers in the early 2000s and the Great Recession in 2008 and 2009, which proved its final undoing.

Borders's first misstep was to invest heavily in CD inventory just as the music industry was revolutionized by digital distribution in the 1990s. As that strategic blunder became apparent, Borders's misstep turned to cognitive paralysis in 2001, when it decided to cede its entire online presence to Amazon just as the day of online was dawning. A quote from the company's 2000 annual report offers a glimpse into its thinking: "Our online investment will be channeled to support our in-store platform, while Borders.com will continue to be utilized as a convenience retail channel."[13]

So instead of recognizing online as the future of retail, the company viewed it as a nuisance, focused solely on its in-store experience, and handed its web presence over to what would become its largest competitor.[14]

Borders's hypoactivity further became apparent through its painfully slow movement in forging a partnership with a coffee partner to give shoppers one more reason to visit its stores. As Barnes and Noble locked the golden goose (Starbucks) into an exclusive contract, the slow-moving Borders was forced to work with second-tier coffee brand Seattle's Best.[15]

Borders's sloth-like movement was even more pronounced on e-readers. Amazon released the Kindle in 2007, Barnes and Noble responded with the Nook in 2009, and then Apple released its juggernaut, the iPad, in April 2010. It wasn't until May of 2010 that Borders finally released the Kobo, an obscure and underperforming entrant in the e-reader category.[16]

Borders was finally done in by the Great Recession. Its inventory became an albatross when it found itself in a cash-poor position under the weight of significant debt. Borders also held misguided long-term leases on many of its unprofitable stores, making downsizing impossible.[17]

By the time the retail giant closed its remaining 399 stores and laid off nearly 11,000 employees, investors had already written it off as dead. Commenting on Borders's demise, Tyler Cowen, economist at George Mason University, said, "Not one single investor, in the whole wide world, thought Borders had a real economic future."[18] It turns out that molasses doesn't make money.

Wild Brands Act Like Broken Records

The second type of crisis-driven inconsistency is stereotypical behavior[19] and perseveration.[20] Both are marked by irrational repetition. Where stereotypical behavior manifests itself in repetitive physical movements, perseveration is seen in repetitive thoughts or words. According to the *Miller-Keane Encyclopedia and Dictionary of Medicine, Nursing, and Allied Health*, perseveration is "the inappropriate persistence . . . of a thought or action after the causative stimulus has ceased."[21] Think of someone who initially answers a question correctly, then continues to provide the same (now incorrect) answer to subsequent questions.

In business, brands can act like broken records by fixating on strategies that once made them successful even though circumstances have changed. Blockbuster, the home video retail juggernaut, happened to love vinyl. The popular explanation for Blockbuster's turbulent fall is to blame Netflix. But a closer look reveals a successful brand that, despite honest attempts to evolve, couldn't resist the sound of its own broken record.

At its height in 2004, Blockbuster ran nearly 9,000 stores, employed nearly 80,000 people, and enjoyed $8 billion in annual revenue.[22] The decisions that led to the brand's infamous bankruptcy actually began nearly a decade earlier when Hollywood faced a record decline in box office revenue in the 1990s.[23] As a downstream home video retailer, Blockbuster's traffic suffered.

Instead of recognizing the permanent shifts in consumer behavior, Blockbuster doubled down on its in-store experience, betting that consumers valued the in-person visit over the entertainment it facilitated. The company brought in a host of executives from 7–11 and, in the words of marketing commentator (and one-time employee of the retailer), Jonathan Salem Baskin, "Blockbuster was reimagined as a convenience store."[24]

Famously, Blockbuster had the opportunity to purchase Netflix for $50 million in 2000, which it declined in favor of a twenty-year on-demand contract with Enron Broadband Services. Enron filed for bankruptcy in 2001.[25]

Finally recognizing the threat of digital, the company's formidable CEO, John Antioco, launched Blockbuster's own online subscription service in 2004 and followed the move by eliminating its highly profitable (but resented) late fees in 2005. By 2006, the company enjoyed two million subscribers and was on its way to managing the upheaval in its business model. But the cost of the investments was high—totaling roughly $400 million[26]—and a growing number of internal stakeholders began plotting moves to undermine the CEO.

Activist investor Carl Icahn orchestrated a takeover of the board and managed to force Antioco out during a contentious period between 2005 and 2007. The subsequent CEO, an internal hire, reversed the no-late-fees policy, increased the online subscription service fees, cut marketing, and renewed the chain's focus on the in-store experience.

One fourth of the subscribers left Blockbuster's online service in the third quarter of 2007 alone, and by 2010, the company filed for bankruptcy. Like a broken record, Blockbuster couldn't help but skip back to its old ways.

Wild Brands Foster Frenzy

According to Leach, the final inconsistent behavior that manifests itself in stressful situations is hyperactivity. *The U.S. National Library of Medicine* describes hyperactivity as a state of heighted activity that includes "impulsiveness," "a shorter attention span," and an "inability concentrating."[27]

Burger King, the consistently inconsistent fast food giant, has made frenzy the rule more than the exception. Notable for a revolving door of ownership groups, C-suite executives, and advertising agencies, Burger King's history of hyperactivity actually dates back decades.

After founding the successful burger chain in the 1950s, founders James McLamore and David R. Edgerton sold the company to Pillsbury in 1967. Following two decades of growth, decline, and upheaval, Pillsbury sold Burger King to Grand Metropolitan, which subsequently merged with Guinness. Burger King was then sold to TPG Capital in 2002, which started a successful five-year growth period that coincided with ad agency Crispin Porter + Bogusky's famous Creepy King advertising campaign focused on the chain's young male core audience.[28]

When growth again declined in 2010, Burger King was sold to 3G Partners.[29] A short period of renewed growth was followed by declining sales, prompting yet another ownership change via a merger with Canadian donut purveyor Tim Hortons.[30]

Sweeping changes in company leadership,[31] marketing partners,[32] and advertising campaigns accompanied each change in ownership, making Burger King something of a byword in its industry.

Burger King's frenzy is especially apparent in a string of copycat menu items and terribly contrived promotions. Jim Vorel, writing for *Paste Magazine*, identifies the worst offenders as the Big King sandwich (an obvious knock off of McDonald's Big Mac, complete with a bun in the middle), a BBQ rib sandwich "meant to imitate McDonald's McRib,"[33] and crispy chicken wraps that are startlingly similar to McDonald's product.

In the midst of its sustained flurry of inconsistency, Burger King slipped to number three in market share behind McDonald's and Wendy's for the first time in forty years.[34]

From Bad to Worse

If the common psychological behaviors experienced under pressure aren't bad enough, there are a number of conditions that can make the situation worse. Knowing how you will react when you find yourself in The Wild is the first step to overcoming inconsistency; understanding the common conditions that push brands farther down the "F" death spiral is the second. These conditions include perpetual impatience, scapegoating, people change, and underlying structural problems, and they represent destructive threats in already dangerous situations.

Perpetual impatience is a plague that afflicts every publicly traded company. Quarterly earnings drive short-term thinking and cause executive tenures to be measured in months instead of years. This can effectively institutionalize inconsistency and incentivize disloyalty and silver-bullet thinking.

Blockbuster's demise is a classic case of perpetual impatience, as investors refused to endure the investment required to ensure Blockbuster's subscription service succeeded and learn to survive without late fees. The short-term thinking led to a customer exodus as the market shifted toward brands that put their customers first.

In addition to perpetual impatience, when brands run into turbulent times, it means the blame game isn't far behind. The Andes crash survivors faced this phenomenon as the desperate days drew into weeks. Politics seeped into the group dynamics like the penetrating cold. Every action was scrutinized, and otherwise blameless members were singled out for unfair accusations and retribution. People turned inward and considered their own well-being before the group's, and a cloud seemed to develop over the stranded passengers. Piers Paul Read, author of *Alive*, summed up the situation: "It was a dangerous mood. A group in stress looks for a scapegoat."[35]

In many ways, John Antioco, CEO of Blockbuster, was a victim of scapegoating. As he courageously led the investment in Blockbuster's online subscription service and eliminated outdated and unfriendly policies like charging late fees, one of his subordinates was fostering an insurrection. The up-and-coming executive John Keyes secretly questioned the high costs of both moves and was a part of the corporate coup. It comes as no surprise that Keyes benefited by becoming CEO not long after. Keyes also holds the honor of leading the ailing brand straight toward bankruptcy.[36]

People change is a normal and potentially healthy part of business. But a culture of perpetual impatience and scapegoating or the onset of hard times can cause people change to increase, resulting in costly turnover, the loss of historical organizational knowledge, constant strategic shifts, and a revolving door of partners and vendors. People change is a particular challenge in that it can be both a result of inconsistency and something that exacerbates it.

One of Burger King's fundamental problems is its repeated people change. With every ownership change came sweeping leadership changes that trickled down through departments and external partners. Every new leader, regardless of skill or expertise, brought fresh ideas and ambitions. Normally, a fresh perspective can provide invaluable insight and energy, but when that's all you have, consistency is impossible, and change becomes an albatross.

The final and most frustrating condition that pushes brands down the "F" death spiral is underlying structural issues. While Burger King can point to a number of issues that hindered its ability to be consistent, from constant ownership changes to formidable headwinds in a changing industry, it has also had to face a lingering structural issue.

Unlike McDonald's, which owns the land its locations sit upon and leases it back to the franchisees, Burger King's franchisees own their own land.[37] This arrangement weakens the corporate leverage needed to keep franchisees aligned. This underscores the fact that, while consistency is a major contributor to a brand's success, underlying structural issues can undermine even smart strategic moves.

Survival in the Andes

Five days after crashing into a remote region of the Andes, the surviving passengers took stock of their situation. Many sat stunned, useless to the group. The rugby players hoped to find some leadership from the only surviving flight crew member, but he was in the worst shape, having lost all control of his bodily functions and weeping uncontrollably.[38] Most knew that they could not go on much longer on their meager daily ration of "a scrap of chocolate, a capful of wine and a teaspoonful of jam or canned fish."[39]

A handful of the young men decided to attempt a hike in search of the tail of the plane. As the aircraft's fuselage shrank into the distance and the remaining survivors became specks in the valley below, every step in the deep snow became a growing struggle. It had been five days since they had had anything substantial to eat, and the bitter cold mixed with the thin mountain air made every effort feel monumental. Having reached their limit, the hikers returned to the fuselage after failing to find any trace of the aircraft's tail.

Contemplating the food supply along their journey, one of the rugby player's named Carlitos Rodriguez vocalized what many of the boys were thinking, documented in *Alive*: " 'Do you know what Nando said to me?' Carlitos said to Fito. 'He said that if we weren't rescued, he'd eat one of the pilots to get out of here.' "[40]

By the tenth day on the mountain, the barren environment and quickly diminishing supplies weren't enough to sustain the remaining twenty-seven survivors. Whispers spread about what must be done, and two different schools of thought arose. A group meeting was finally called to openly debate the topic.[41]

The deeply religious rugby team struggled mightily, but after an extended discussion, a decision was made. Silence swept over the group as they sat like stone. Finally, four players quietly stood up and walked outside.

The freezing temperatures had served as a perfect preservation method of the deceased passengers. One of the four boys, a young man named Roberto Canessa, knelt down beside the selected body. He cut deep into the flesh using a broken shard of glass, removing twenty slivers and placing them on top of the fuselage to bake in the sun.[42]

Then they sat in silence. No one could muster the courage to do what came next until Canessa walked over to the meat and took it in his hand. Struggling as if moving through honey, he placed the meat in his mouth and swallowed. Slowly, one by one, most of the others followed suit. Only a few could not take the plunge.[43]

The next morning, some of the players were able to get the plane's radio to receive incoming signals, and they listened intently for any news of rescue. *Alive* documents what they heard next. The radio announcer's statement read like a punch to the gut: "This follows the cancellation of the search by the SAR for the Uruguayan aircraft because of negative results."[44]

The boys wept.

All except one. Upon hearing the news, Nando Parrado quietly stared at the mountains to the west. He knew what must be done.

As both our research and the amazing story of the Andes survivors attest, The Wild can turn even the most civilized companies wild. As the limbic system takes control, behavior becomes erratic. Without an intervention, even the best brands can get stuck bouncing between fight-flight-freeze reactions until finally succumbing to the "F" death spiral.

But that doesn't have to be your story. Just as Parrado looked to the mountains and knew there had to be another way, you can find hope and turn your brand around. But as you'll read in Chapter 5, before things get better, they sometimes get worse.

Survival Tips for Practical Application

Erratic behavior is a sign of a lost brand, but it doesn't have to stay that way.

Keep in Mind

- Inconsistency is the third internal dynamic brands wrestle with when they are lost in the wilderness.
- Logic is elusive when the limbic system takes over in stressful situations.
- Brands that can't overcome erratic behavior in the impact and recovery phases fall into the "F" death spiral, never moving on to the rescue and post-trauma phases.

Survival Tips

To navigate The Wild:

- Identify where you fall in the three categories of inconsistent behaviors: moving like molasses, acting like a broken record, or fostering frenzy.
- Intervene in the common conditions that can make inconsistency worse: perpetual impatience, scapegoating, people change, and lingering structural problems.

Notes

1. Piers Paul Read, *Alive: Sixteen Men, Seventy-Two Days, and Insurmountable Odds—the Classic Adventure of Survival in the Andes* (New York: Harper Perennial, 2005), 25–32, 45.
2. Steve McKee, *When Growth Stalls: How It Happens, Why You're Stuck, and What to Do about It* (San Francisco: Jossey-Bass, 2009), 92.
3. Brad Fitzpatrick, "Your Brain on Survival: Here's What Happens When the Body Shifts into Survival Mode, and How You Can Stay in Control," *Outdoor Life*, 223, no. 3 (April 2016), 47.
4. Rand Swenson, "Chapter 9-Limbic System," in *Review of Clinical and Functional Neuroscience-Swenson*, 2006, accessed August 5, 2016, http://www.dartmouth.edu/%7Erswenson/NeuroSci/chapter_9.html.
5. Swenson, "Chapter 9-Limbic System."
6. Michael Ray Taylor, *Cave Passages: Roaming the Underground Wilderness* (New York: Vintage Books, 1997), 24.
7. *The Free Dictionary,* s.v. "Nitrogen Narcosis," accessed July 2, 2016, http://medical-dictionary.thefreedictionary.com/nitrogen+narcosis.
8. John Leach, "Survival Psychology: The Won't to Live." *The Psychologist.com*, January 2011, https://thepsychologist.bps.org.uk/volume-24/edition-1/survival-psychology-wont-live.
9. Richard Simon and Martin Forstenzer, "Pilot Hikes 9 Days over Sierra after Crash," *Los Angeles Times*, December 10, 1994, http://articles.latimes.com/1994–12–10/local/me-7204_1_inyo-county.
10. Leach, "Survival Psychology: The Won't to Live."
11. *The Free Dictionary,* s.v. "Hypoactivity," accessed July 2, 2016, http://medical-dictionary.thefreedictionary.com/hypoactivity.
12. Read, *Alive,* 143–144.
13. *Borders Group 2000 Annual Report*, PDF (Borders Group Inc., 2000), 7.
14. Annie Lowrey, "Readers without Borders: What Killed the Big-Box Retailer? Hint: It Wasn't the Internet," *Slate*, July 20, 2011, http://www.slate.com/articles/business/moneybox/2011/07/readers_without_borders.html.
15. Lowrey, "Readers without Borders: What Killed the Big-Box Retailer? Hint: It Wasn't the Internet."
16. Lowrey, "Readers without Borders: What Killed the Big-Box Retailer? Hint: It Wasn't the Internet."

17. Josh Sanburn, "5 Reasons Borders Went Out of Business (and What Will Take Its Place)," *Time*, July 19, 2011, http://business.time.com/2011/07/19/5-reasons-borders-went-out-of-business-and-what-will-take-its-place/.

18. Tyler Cowen, Twitter post, July 18, 2011, https://twitter.com/tylercowen/status/93068004870471681.

19. *Dictionary.com Unabridged,* s.v. "stereotypy," Dictionary.com, Random House, accessed October 18, 2016, http://www.dictionary.com/browse/stereotypy.

20. *Miller-Keane Encyclopedia and Dictionary of Medicine, Nursing, and Allied Health, Seventh Edition,* s.v. "perseveration," accessed October 18, 2016, http://medical-dictionary.thefreedictionary.com/perseveration.

21. *Miller-Keane Encyclopedia and Dictionary of Medicine, Nursing, and Allied Health, Seventh Edition,* s.v. "perseveration,"

22. Paula Bernstein, "Did Netflix Really Put Blockbuster Out of Business? This Infographic Tells the Story," *IndieWire.com*, February 4, 2014, http://www.indiewire.com/2014/02/did-netflix-really-put-blockbuster-out-of-business-this-infographic-tells-the-story-30351/.

23. Jonathan Salem Baskin, "The Internet Didn't Kill Blockbuster, the Company Did It to Itself," *Forbes*, November 8, 2013, http://www.forbes.com/sites/jonathansalembaskin/2013/11/08/the-internet-didnt-kill-blockbuster-the-company-did-it-to-itself/#4e1f69fd13c1.

24. Salem Baskin, "The Internet Didn't Kill Blockbuster, the Company Did It to Itself."

25. Salem Baskin, "The Internet Didn't Kill Blockbuster, the Company Did It to Itself."

26. Greg Satell, "A Look Back at Why Blockbuster Really Failed and Why It Didn't Have to," *Forbes*, September 5, 2014, 1–2, http://www.forbes.com/sites/gregsatell/2014/09/05/a-look-back-at-why-blockbuster-really-failed-and-why-it-didnt-have-to/2/#60f686613a2f.

27. *MedlinePlus,* s.v. "Hyperactivity," accessed August 3, 2016, https://medlineplus.gov/ency/article/003256.htm.

28. Julie Jargon, "As Sales Drop, Burger King Draws Critics for Courting 'Super Fans'," *The Wall Street Journal*, February 1, 2010, http://www.wsj.com/articles/SB10001424052748703410004575029130114102118.

29. Rick Aristotle Munarriz, "Fast Food's Slow Fail: Why Burger King Will Never Be Great Again," *AOL.com,* April 4, 2012, http://www.aol.com/

article/2012/04/04/fast-food-slow-fail-why-burger-king-will-never-be-great-again/20208467/.

30. Dan Myers, "10 Things You Didn't Know about Burger King," *The Huffingtonpost.com*, May 22, 2016, http://www.huffingtonpost.com/the-daily-meal/10-things-you-didnt-know-about-burger-king_b_7317582.html.

31. Maureen Morrison, "Burger King Names David Lead Global Agency: Chain Worked with Shop in Brazil, Argentina and Parts of the U.S.," *Advertising Age*, April 28, 2014, http://adage.com/article/agency-news/burger-king-names-david-lead-global-agency/292914/; The Associated Press, "Burger King Changes Slogan to 'Be Your Way'," *New York Daily News*, May 19, 2014, http://www.nydailynews.com/life-style/eats/burger-king-slogan-article-1.1798278; Maureen Morrison, "Burger King Beefs up Agency Roster with Mother, David," *Advertising Age*, January 11, 2012, http://adage.com/article/agency-news/burger-king-beefs-ad-agency-roster-mother-david/232046/.

32. Maureen Morrison, "Burger King Splits with Lead Agency Mother: Creative Differences Cited as Reason for Latest in String of Agency Partings," *Advertising Age*, January 6, 2014, http://adage.com/article/agency-news/burger-king-splits-lead-agency-mother/290931/.

33. Jim Vorel, "Eating Badly: Burger Kind, The Saddest Chain in Fast Food," *Paste*, January 19, 2015, https://www.pastemagazine.com/articles/2015/01/eating-badly-burger-king-the-saddest-chain-in-fast.html.

34. Vorel, "Eating Badly: Burger Kind, The Saddest Chain in Fast Food"; Morrison, "Burger King Beefs up Agency Roster with Mother, David."

35. Read, *Alive*, 152.

36. Satell, "A Look Back at Why Blockbuster Really Failed and Why It Didn't Have to."

37. Cliff Kuang, "Burger King's Struggling: Is Their Ad Agency to Blame?" *Fast Company*, June 23, 2009, http://www.fastcompany.com/1299137/burger-kings-struggling-their-ad-agency-blame.

38. Read, *Alive*, 45.

39. Read, *Alive*, 77.

40. Read, *Alive*, 60.

41. Read, *Alive*, 78–79.

42. Read, *Alive*, 81.

43. Read, *Alive*, 82.

44. Read, *Alive*, 85.

CHAPTER 5

Savage

"Under such conditions," Roosevelt wrote, "whatever is evil in men's natures comes to the front."[1]

—Candice Millard, *The River of Doubt*

Julio de Lima slunk away from the others at the first opportunity. The jungle's oppressive heat and impossible rapids made for another burdensome day for former U.S. president Teddy Roosevelt's expedition. The formidable Amazon river tributary known as the River of Doubt had worn down the bodies and minds of the besieged group of men and made Roosevelt's 1914 expedition to explore the uncharted waterway an exercise in suffering. While the group was struggling to transport its food supplies from the previous night's camp, Julio slipped his hands into a package of dried meat, one of the expedition's most precious stores.

A trusted underling caught Julio in the act and reported him to a respected officer named Paishon. It wasn't the first time Julio had stolen from the starving expedition. He had been caught once before, so the expedition officers knew of his character flaw. He couldn't even be trusted to join others to scavenge for food, as everyone knew he would immediately devour anything he found.

In such extreme conditions, isolated from civilization, there was little they could do beyond reprimanding Julio. According to Candice Millard in *The River of Doubt*, Roosevelt privately feared open mutiny as supplies dwindled and the expedition plunged ever deeper into the endless jungle.[2] The officers were outnumbered, and rising tensions kept the group splintered.

As the day's journey continued, Julio struggled to carry his share of the weight up the steep hills. A frustrated Paishon openly and repeatedly rebuked him.

Later, Roosevelt and two officers watched as Julio slowly walked into camp complaining about the weight of his load. Julio lowered his pack to the ground and casually walked over to the rifles. The others were encouraged, hoping Julio had caught site of a rare beast they might enjoy for dinner.

Minutes later they heard a shot. Roosevelt asked what animal Julio had killed. The others were speculating when they saw three men rushing through the jungle toward camp. Millard documented what happened next.

" '*Julio mato Paishon!*' they shouted in Portuguese. 'Julio has killed Paishon!' "[3]

Much like the desperate members of Roosevelt's expedition, after descending from fear to drift to inconsistency, lost brands will turn savage. Debilitating fear and the frustration of failure, mixed with aimlessness and despair, can result in even close companions turning on one another. It is both the most expected and ugliest aspect of The Wild.

According to our research, embattled companies lack any semblance of alignment. They struggle with making critical decisions and are three times more likely than healthy companies to experience internal discord. Lost brands are also four times more likely to say various team members are moving in different directions and are six times less likely to report that they know where their company is going.[4]

Savage brands don't start that way. As long as revenue and margins are growing, internal disagreements are easy to ignore. But, as Millard noted in *The River of Doubt*, "great difficulty often [brings] out the worst in a man."[5] Growing external pressures cause festering internal disagreement to finally erupt. Employees turn inward, disillusioned with colleagues and hopeless about the future. Trust breaks down. Then an enduring law of The Wild, Every Person for Himself, devours everything.

In extreme scenarios, internal discord saps much-needed strength, distracts the team when focus is needed most, and can lead to a form of brand suicide. When experiencing discord firsthand, hope that things will get better can be elusive. A closer look at the study of group dynamics and game theory reveals what's really going on and demonstrates that even in the darkest hour, there is always a way to turn things around.

One of the common self-deceptions a savage brand falls into is the belief that success is a zero-sum game. The *Merriam-Webster Dictionary* defines zero-sum as "a situation (as a game or relationship) in which a gain for one side entails a corresponding loss for the other side."[6]

A notable example of zero-sum in game theory is Matching Pennies. Matching Pennies is a contest in which two players are each given a penny and told to turn them over at the same time. One player is told that if she can match the other player's side of the coin, either heads or tails, she receives a point. The other player is told that if she is able to choose the opposite side of the coin from her opponent, she receives a point. Thus, neither player can win unless the other loses, and both are incentivized to compete rather than cooperate.[7]

The easiest way to visualize zero-sum is through a payoff matrix, a basic chart used in game theory to analyze different scenarios. In the example that follows, a score of 1 represents a win and a score of -1 represents a loss. No scenario facilitates a win for both players.

Julio de Lima fell for the zero-sum lie as he put his own needs above the others' and refused to share with his expedition companions. As the lie took hold, Julio's selfishness manifested itself first in deception, then in theft, and finally in murder.

By 1993, IBM had turned savage. The company found itself entrenched in a zero-sum culture built on an individualistic sales force that had driven the organization's success through the 1960s and 1970s.[8] By the 1990s, the zero-sum game was unsustainable, and IBM was in trouble.

Matching Pennies

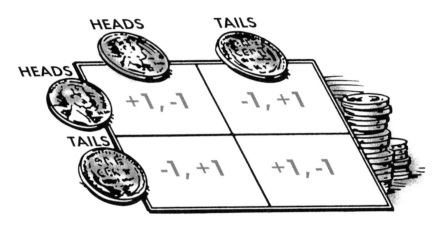

Figure 5.1   *Matching Pennies*

As the company faced annual losses measured in billions, it continued to rely on sales of mainframes, which were thought to be under siege by personal computers.[9] Wharton reported that by 1993, the business world had come to a general consensus that IBM was done for, exemplified by Oracle's Larry Ellison quipping, "IBM? We don't even think about those guys anymore. They're not dead, but they're irrelevant."[10]

Famously, Lou Gerstner was brought in as CEO to steer the ailing company back to growth. When Gerstner first arrived, he focused entirely on strategy but soon found that culture was his primary challenge. Harvard Business School reported that "In his first three months on the job, he didn't spend 'an hour' thinking about culture."[11] But Gerstner quickly discovered that while strategy was important, changing the culture was his first task. Writing in *Who Says Elephants Can't Dance*, Gerstner said "Culture isn't just one aspect of the game. . . . It is the game."[12]

Upon arriving at IBM, Gerstner found that he wasn't running an integrated company focused on customers but instead a series of warring fiefdoms perpetually arguing with one another over internal pricing and processes. He battled with managers who refused to share his regular email updates with their teams, found business units bickering and hiding information from one another, and watched as a legacy zero-sum culture hindered IBM from moving toward a team-based future.[13]

One method to move beyond zero-sum cultures is to recast internal success as a choice between individual mediocrity and mutual gain. A game theory example is known as Stag Hunt. In Stag Hunt, two players must separately choose to either hunt a stag, which is worth 2 points, or a hare, which is worth 1 point. If either player chooses to hunt the hare, they are ensured a single point. But to successfully hunt the more valuable stag, players must work together.

In Stag Hunt, three outcomes are possible. One player gets nothing while the other gains a point; both players gain a single point; or both players score two points through cooperation. The difficulty is that mutual gain requires a suppression of rational selfishness. Individually, it is easier and more logical to go for the sure thing. To hunt the stag, players must trust that the other player will act just as unselfishly as they do.

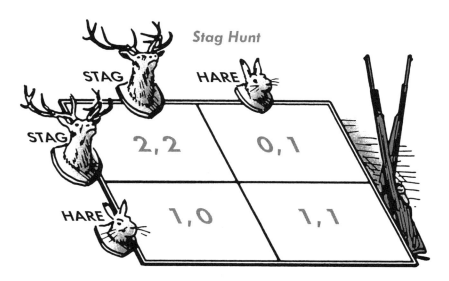

Figure 5.2 *Stag Hunt*

As Gerstner took the helm at IBM, his first job was to shift the culture from one in which zero-sum thinking was the norm to one in which cooperation prevailed. In 1993, the corporation had been planning to splinter into many smaller, more agile companies. But Gerstner had a different plan. To turn around the juggernaut and "make the elephant dance," Gerstner refocused the company on integration and services and away from hardware and software. He created a new pricing structure for customers that removed internal transfer fees and did something unthinkable to many at the time: he allowed IBM consultants to recommend competitor hardware and software solutions if they made more sense for customers.

Before it could accomplish integration for clients, IBM had to first become integrated itself. In a speech to MBA students at Harvard Business School recounting the effort, Gerstner said, "We needed to integrate as a team inside the company so that we could integrate for the customers on their premises. It flew in the face of what everybody did in their careers before I arrived there."[14]

Mutual Gain or Mutually Assured Mediocrity

Fundamentally, management teams in the brand wilderness face a choice between two eventual outcomes: mutual gain or mutually assured mediocrity. In game theory, this is called a Nash Equilibrium. John Nash, the mathematical genius depicted in the 2001 film *A Beautiful Mind*, coined the term while developing his theory of noncooperative games in the 1950s, work that would eventually lead to a Nobel Prize.[15]

Kenneth Chang, writing for the *New York Times*, describes a Nash Equilibrium as "a stable state in which no player can gain advantage through a unilateral change of strategy, assuming the others do not change what they are doing."[16] Essentially, if a player can't improve his situation without another player changing his, you have reached Nash Equilibrium.

In the Stag Hunt example, if both players choose to hunt a hare, both receive the lesser reward, and neither can benefit by hunting the more

Nash Equilibrium

Figure 5.3 *Nash Equilibrium*

valuable stag. For brands lost in the wilderness, I call this stage of mutually assured mediocrity "Savage Equilibrium." The list of brands suffering from Savage Equilibrium is long and ignominious and has included
IBM, Kodak, Staples, Blockbuster, and many more. As long as employees can't achieve a greater benefit by acting unselfishly, Savage Equilibrium creates a destructive form of stalemate.

Conversely, brands that find a way to overcome discord and unite in
purpose and action can achieve the positive state of mutual gain known
as "Noble Equilibrium." Noble Equilibrium is a rarer outcome because
employees must become convinced that greater reward is possible through
cooperation. They must be culturally incentivized to choose this course of
action and trust that their colleagues will choose unselfishly at the same time.

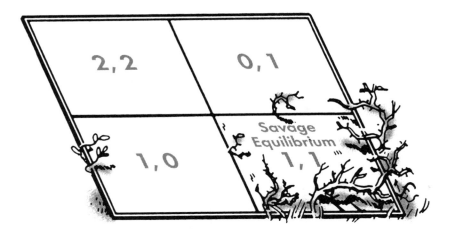

Figure 5.4   *Savage Equilibrium*

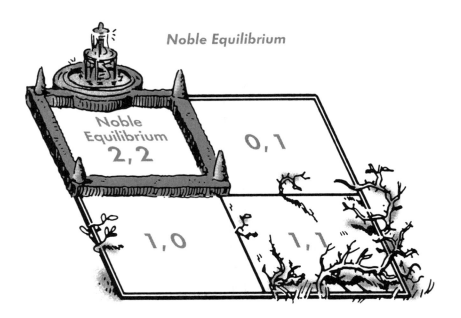

Figure 5.5   *Noble Equilibrium*

In the Noble and Savage paradigm, every employee decision is either moving the organization toward Noble Equilibrium or toward Savage Equilibrium. Every choice counts. Nothing is static. Either trust and unity drive decisions toward mutual gain, or shortsightedness and fear create mutually assured mediocrity.

Whether a decision moves the organization closer to Noble Equilibrium or Savage Equilibrium is determined by the cultural incentives in place as well as by leadership's reinforcement of those incentives. During Lou Gerstner's journey with IBM, he considered the importance of incentives, writing, "What does the culture reward and punish—individual achievement or team play, risk taking or consensus building?" If you seek more than a Savage Equilibrium for your management team, you'll find out what you're incentivizing fast.

Savage Equilibrium comes about in many ways, and often the more extreme the situation, the pettier the stalemate. In 1967, four expert climbers set out to complete the first winter ascent of Mount McKinley. The expedition was so daring that many wrote it off as a fantasy. Early in the climb, the expedition suffered a major setback as their most seasoned climber fell into a crevasse and died. Horrified, the climbers almost turned back but instead chose to push on.

The expedition eventually reached the summit, but on the descent, a freak windstorm trapped the three remaining climbers in a hand-dug snow cave for six desperate nights. Forced to cook in the same tin can they urinated into, the trio desperately fought against starvation, frostbite, and the violent storm.

As one of the climbers, Art Davidson, lay in his sleeping bag trying to keep his feet warm in down booties, he noticed but ignored his friend's quiet whimpers. Ray, a fellow climber, complained of swollen hands, a sure sign of the beginning of frostbite. But because Ray had no booties, his feet were even worse than his hands. Art later commented on the ordeal, writing about the interaction with Ray in *Minus 148*, "he asked about my down booties. Though he didn't say it outright, I could tell he wanted to wear them. I tried to ignore him, acting as if I hadn't heard."[17]

As the days drew on, the situation became dire. It had been thirty-six hours since the trio drank water. Dehydration in the subzero temperatures caused their circulation to slow, exacerbating the frostbite. To get water, the climbers needed gas to melt the snow, which meant that one of them would have to leave the cave and brave the windstorm in order to retrieve a cached gallon of gas placed nearby three years earlier. No one knew if the climber who left for the gas would make it back to the cave.

Art felt that because of his swollen hands, he was unable to go. Yet he couldn't bring himself to ask his companions. Instead, he wrote that he chose to "lay quietly in my bag, letting my silence ask someone else to go." In the misery of slow death, no one moved. Welcome to Savage Equilibrium.

Finally, an act of selflessness broke the stalemate. Ray quietly got out of his sleeping bag and tried to put on his boots, but his feet were swollen so badly that he couldn't get them on, so Art offered his down booties to Ray for the dreadful trip to the cache.

Ray waited by the entrance for a lull in the fierce wind. At the perfect moment, he lurched out of the cave with a grunt. Fifteen minutes passed, far longer than was needed to retrieve the buried gas. Art knew the trip was dangerous, and now he began considering what he would do if Ray never returned.

Minutes later, dread turned to joy as a can of gas tumbled into the cave. A numb Ray stumbled in behind, unable to feel his feet. The over-joyed survivors lit the flame, melted the ice, and slaked their thirst with warm water.

Ray didn't offer the booties back to Art, but Art was so appreciative of the gas and subsequent water that he didn't even ask for them. Later, in another moment of altruism, Ray offered a single booty to Art so that they could both at least share some comfort. Art would call it "the most touching thing I had ever seen (Ray) do."[18]

After six days in the ice cave, the winds died down enough for the nearly dead climbers to attempt to descend the mountain, marking one of the most harrowing climbing stories of all time. Every man survived the return trip, though many ended up losing fingers and toes due to the extreme frostbite.

JCPenney's Mutually Assured Mediocrity

JCPenney wallowed in mutually assured mediocrity during a period of "transformation" at the end of 2011 when it hired Apple retail sweetheart Ron Johnson as CEO. While many point to flawed strategy as the chief reason Johnson failed to turn the retail giant around, a more sophisticated understanding shows how a lack of consensus pulled JCPenney into a Savage Equilibrium.

Despite being talented and creative, Ron Johnson failed at JCPenney, though the company's decline didn't come as a result of bad ideas but because of a cultural blind spot and the devastating effects of internal discord. In the midst of struggling sales at the embattled retailer, Johnson sent mixed messages to employees by spending $170 million on recruiting and moving three new top executives onto the JCPenney leadership team.[19] The recruitment of outsiders led to an insular environment at the top, with legacy employees shut out.[20]

Johnson jolted longtime employees by foisting an Apple-esque culture onto the traditional retailer, then pummeled morale with layoffs. In a sign that Johnson subconsciously may not have completely believed in Penney's transformation, he never moved to the retailer's headquarters in Plano, Texas, choosing instead to commute from his home in California.[21]

Remaining legacy employees had little incentive to do more than what was required of them as Johnson and his army of "outsiders" attempted to remake the brand and experience. While Johnson and crew aimed for the stag, JCPenney employees settled for the hare.

Noel Tichy summed up the cultural disaster in a *Fortune* article when he wrote, "The cost . . . could be measured not just in dollars but in the incalculable cost of declining morale that blowing up the existing hierarchy in the name of transformation rang up on the chain's internal registers."

As you fight internal discord and the savage results of a lack of consensus, several common mistakes can hinder your ability to find your way out. The first pitfall is to discount consensus in the first place. A choir of experts and consultants disparage consensus as the enemy of progress. For example, Mike Myatt, writing in *Forbes,* called consensus "devastating to all things productive," "team-building's silent killer," and the "assassin of culture."[22] That may be true if you define consensus as "everyone agreeing all the time." But such a definition is as unhelpful as it is impossible. Instead, understand consensus as general agreement built on internal buy-in, common purpose, alignment of incentives, and an unselfish focus on the "stag." In this definition, consensus doesn't mean lockstep agreement, but it does require a commitment to arriving at a common understanding, combined with strong leadership. Those who continue to focus on the "hare" can (and should) leave. Those who remain can then move productively in the same direction.

Another common blunder is for a leader to assume a consensus that doesn't really exist. In psychology, this phenomenon is called the False Consensus Effect. The False Consensus Effect is the inclination we all have to overestimate how much other people agree with us.[23] Ron Johnson may have fallen victim to the False Consensus Effect in his failed turnaround efforts. While his vision was arguably exactly the change the discount-addicted retail industry needed, he underestimated the confusion of legacy JCPenney employees and their resistance to the new direction.

A subtler but more dangerous challenge to gaining consensus is a phenomenon in psychology known as pluralistic ignorance. This is a situation in which significant numbers of team members privately disagree with a group decision but publicly go along with it because they assume the majority is in favor.[24] Pluralistic ignorance is dangerous because it leads to a false belief that consensus has been achieved, followed by passive-aggressive behavior toward change.

IBM's Lou Gerstner wrestled with a form of pluralistic ignorance when he discovered that the company's employees in Europe were not receiving his regular email updates. Looking into the matter, he found out that the executive in charge of IBM's European operations was not allowing the emails to go through to employees. According to Wharton's account of the exchange, the executive said that the emails from the company's CEO—his boss—were "inappropriate for his employees."[25] Pluralistic ignorance is hard to diagnose and difficult to root out and is a sure killer of unity.

On the Banks of the Amazon River

Paishon was dead. Julio was on the loose. Despite a festering leg wound and rising fever, Roosevelt leapt to his feet and grabbed a rifle. The entire expedition was terrified that Julio was on a rampage and began a search along the river for the killer on the lam. Not long into the search, they discovered the murder weapon in a thicket near the trail. They assumed it was ripped from Julio's hands in the thicket as he fled the scene of the crime.

As day turned to night, a weight hung over the camp. In the moment, the remaining members of the expedition were united by the horror of murder. But their unity quickly faded as Roosevelt and his chief officer, Cândido Rondon, violently disagreed about how to deal with the murderer. Roosevelt believed swift justice was in order, saying, "Julio has to be tracked, arrested and killed."[26]

Rondon, while irate about the murder, refused to condone any form of wilderness justice, claiming Brazil did not allow for capital punishment. In truth, Rondon had joined the expedition in part to survey the uncharted river and was looking for a reason to delay the journey to enable his work.

Nervous calm returned to the camp as time passed and Julio failed to turn up. The expedition slowly made its way downriver, never resolving how they would deal with Julio if and when he was found. Three days later, a muddy, dark figure appeared along the riverbank. Julio was alive.

But he looked like a shell of his old, muscular self. He desperately called from a tree branch hanging over the river and begged Rondon to let him rejoin the expedition. Three nights alone in the jungle had transformed Julio into something less than human.

Rondon refused to stop the boats but told Roosevelt he intended to send a search party from camp that day. The news created an uproar as Roosevelt and his officers fiercely disagreed. What little unity had been created after the murder had now been completely lost. Roosevelt knew Rondon's true intentions were to buy time to survey the river—time Roosevelt was desperate to use to get out of the jungle. Near death himself and fearful for his own son's safety, Roosevelt wanted nothing more than to leave the forsaken place.

As the party's chief officer, Rondon won the argument and sent a search party to find Julio the next morning. After hiking for an entire day, building campfires, calling out his name, and shooting in the air, the search party returned with no sign of Julio. Rondon had no choice but to move on, leaving Julio to the mercy of the jungle.

The Wild can turn the best of us into professional savages. The descent from paralyzing fear and drift to wild inconsistency and savagery is wrought with pain and despair. The Wild is littered with the remains of well-meaning but misguided management teams. Yet it doesn't have to be that way.

A thorough understanding of survival psychology and our research into the internal and external dynamics that affect growth reveals the destructive forces that harm lost brands. The physiological response to fear and the long slide into the abyss are well documented. Drift dilemma can be overcome. Brands don't have to fall victim to the "F" death spiral. And Savage Equilibrium is not a forgone conclusion.

The path out of the brand wilderness is fraught with danger. But it can be navigated. Armed with an understanding of The Wild, you are now ready to take control, make the tough decisions, and blaze your path to success.

Now get up. Choose to thrive.

Survival Tips for Practical Application

No matter how dark things seem, brands can always choose their own path. Use the tips that follow to diagnose your brand and arm yourself with the knowledge needed to turn things around.

Keep in Mind

- The fourth internal dynamic reported by struggling brands is internal discord.
- The zero-sum lie says your success requires your teammates to lose.
- Reality is closer to the Stag Hunt, in which cooperation leads to shared gain while selfishness leads to mutually assured mediocrity.

Survival Tips

To navigate The Wild:

- Understand that all organizations are perpetually heading toward Noble or Savage Equilibrium.
- Determine which behaviors your culture incentivizes and leadership reinforces.
- Commit to overcoming the dangers of The Wild and choose to thrive.

Notes

1. Candice Millard, *The River of Doubt: Theodore Roosevelt's Darkest Journey* (New York: Anchor Books, 2006), 286.
2. Millard, *The River of Doubt*, 143.
3. Millard, *The River of Doubt*, 287–288.
4. Steve McKee, *When Growth Stalls: How It Happens, Why You're Stuck, and What to Do about It* (San Francisco: Jossey-Bass, 2009), 44.

5. Millard, *The River of Doubt*, 143.

6. *Merriam-Webster,* s.v. "Zero-sum," accessed August 3, 2016, http://www. merriam-webster.com/dictionary/zero%E2%80%93sum.

7. Investopedia Staff, "Matching Pennies," *Investopedia,* accessed August 30, 2016, http://www.investopedia.com/terms/m/matching-pennies.asp.

8. Martha Lagace, "Gerstner: Changing Culture at IBM—Lou Gerstner Discusses Changing the Culture at IBM," *HBS Working Knowledge,* December 9, 2002, http://hbswk.hbs.edu/archive/3209.html.

9. "Lou Gerstner's Turnaround Tales at IBM," Wharton University of Pennsylvania (audio blog), December 18, 2002, http://knowledge.wharton.upenn. edu/article/lou-gerstners-turnaround-tales-at-ibm/.

10. "Lou Gerstner's Turnaround Tales at IBM."

11. Lagace, "Gerstner."

12. Louis V. Gerstener, Jr., *Who Says Elephants Can't Dance? Inside IBM's Historic Turnaround* (New York: Harper Business, 2002), 182.

13. "Lou Gerstner's Turnaround Tales at IBM."

14. Lagace, "Gerstner."

15. Erica Goode, "John F. Nash r., Math Genius Defined by a 'Beautiful Mind,' Dies at 86," *The New York Times*, May 24, 2015, http://www.nytimes. com/2015/05/25/science/john-nash-a-beautiful-mind-subject-and-nobel-winner-dies-at-86.html?_r=0.

16. Kenneth Chang, "Explaining a Cornerstone of Game Theory: John Nash's Equilibrium," *The New York Times*, May 24, 2015, http://www.nytimes. com/2015/05/25/science/explaining-a-cornerstone-of-game-theory-john-nashs-equilibrium.html.

17. Art Davidson, *Minus 148°: First Winter Ascent of Mt. McKinley*, 3rd ed. (Seattle: The Mountaineers, 1999), 169–170.

18. Davidson, *Minus 148°*

19. Noel Tichy, "JCPenney and the Terrible Costs of Hiring an Outsider CEO," *Fortune,* November 13, 2014, http://fortune.com/2014/11/13/jc-penney-ron-johnson-ceo-succession/.

20. Tichy, "JCPenney and the Terrible Costs of Hiring an Outsider CEO."

21. Tichy, "JCPenney and the Terrible Costs of Hiring an Outsider CEO."

22. Mike Myatt, "Consensus- Team Building's Silent Killer," *Forbes*, April 19, 2012, http://www.forbes.com/sites/mikemyatt/2012/04/19/consensus-team-buildings-silent-killer/#4bd6cdf87920.

23. "False Consensus Effect: Definition and Example," *Study.com*, accessed September 13, 2016, http://study.com/academy/lesson/false-consensus-effect-definition-example.html.
24. Pam MS, *Psychology Dictionary,* s.v. "What Is Pluralistic Ignorance?" accessed July 30, 2016, http://psychologydictionary.org/pluralistic-ignorance/.
25. "Lou Gerstner's Turnaround Tales at IBM."
26. Millard, *The River of Doubt*, 291.

CHAPTER 6

Stop

It's very reassuring to know that there is nothing on this earth that we cannot deal with, and there is no place where we cannot survive.[1]
—John Wiseman, *SAS Survival Handbook*

John Sain looked at the trailhead with anticipation. He had been eager to hunt rutting bull elk for months. His pack was filled with everything he needed for the five-mile hike and the following morning's hunt. He grabbed his rifle and hiked to his camping spot in time to set up for the night.

He awoke early and set out to beat the elk to their bedding spot. His fit legs easily carried him across the uneven forest floor. The area was a mess. It had suffered a wildfire years before that weakened the timber and created a natural maze of fallen trees and brush. Though he was a seasoned hunter, Sain was nervous about hiking through the overgrown canyons and unstable brush, but he pushed on in a race with the elk. He needed to arrive at the elks' bedding spot before they did in order to set up the perfect shot.

In what Josh Dahlke, writing for *Outdoor Life*, called "a flash," Sain was in blinding pain.[2] While traversing a tangled mess of fallen trees and branches, he slipped and caught his leg between two logs. He fell forward and immediately snapped both bones in his right leg.

Sain tried to make sense of the situation. Not realizing the extent of his injury, he attempted to stand with the help of a walking stick. As he put weight on his leg, it crumbled, and he collapsed backward, his leg ending up next to his rib cage.

Sain's plight was made worse by his decision not to notify anyone of his whereabouts before departing for the hunt. Located eight miles from his truck with no radio or cell reception, he knew it was over. Stunned and in excruciating pain, the father of two reached for his pistol. With no one aware of his plight and no hope of crawling out of the forest, he decided it would be best to end it all.

Like John Sain, who found himself in unexpected circumstances, every brand will face its form of The Wild at some point in its life cycle. When a brand is alone in the wilderness, suffering from some mix of the four internal dynamics, marketers may feel it's impossible to know where to start.

According to J. Wayne Fears's *The Pocket Outdoor Survival Guide*, when people first realize they are lost in the wilderness, they often panic and drop their packs, begin running, or keep wandering until they find themselves in even worse circumstances. Some have even been known to hide from rescuers.[3]

Fears says people act erratically because of irrational fear of embarrassment, punishment, discomfort, the unknown, being alone, and more.[4] Not surprisingly, these are the same fears business leaders experience when facing their version of The Wild. From the professional shame they may experience after failing or losing their job to the unfair blame they may endure and the dread they feel as stockholders abandon the company, leaders may find the effects of The Wild overwhelming.

It is easy to feel isolated and uncomfortable when you are trying to turn around a lost brand, but the only way to overcome The Wild's ceaseless unknowns is to embrace them. Paradoxically, as your body and mind demand action in a desperate situation, the first thing you should do is nothing. To begin navigating The Wild, you must first stop. S.T.O.P. is, in fact, a common acronym memorized by Boy Scouts and survivalists across the world.[5]

Sit
Think
Observe
Plan

The core challenge in survival situations is that—no matter what you know, how you've trained, or what resources you have available—nothing matters if your mind is in the wrong place. Or, as Dahlke put it in *Outdoor Life*, "When ordinary people find themselves in extraordinary circumstances, survival becomes a state of mind."[6]

Sitting still in an extreme situation is counterintuitive and requires every ounce of your will. The act of stopping and quieting your mind is just what you don't want to do. Yet you must. Stopping is the beginning of the journey to overcome fear—not to eliminate it or beat it but to act in spite of it. In other words, stopping is your first act of courage.

Courage is not the absence of fear. In fact, courage can't exist without fear. The *Merriam-Webster Dictionary* calls courage "the ability to do something that you know is difficult or dangerous."[7] The *Oxford Dictionary* goes further and calls it "strength in the face of pain or grief."[8]

Stopping in a crisis is unnatural. When grappling with a difficult challenge, your mind and body scream for action. Every chemical, hormone, and brain signal is preprogrammed to force you into activity. Yet by choosing to stop and sit, literally and metaphorically, you're allowing your frontal lobe to begin retaking control from your limbic system. This simple action, while small in scale, is profound in importance.

In the midst of an overwhelming situation, the purposeful act of sitting is your first opportunity to exert control over the uncontrollable. Your moment of stillness allows you to think instead of just feel. As you give yourself permission to think, you begin restoring logic and rationality.

Experts point to a number of vital mental actions survivors must take during this self-imposed stillness in order to find and regain the right state of mind. These actions can be summed up in three steps: people who navigate The Wild admit that they are lost, they submit to reality, and they commit to live.

These three steps, though simple, must not be discounted. They are deceptively small in scale, yet they can be the difference between life and death.

Admit You Are Lost

Admitting you are lost sounds straightforward, but in the midst of a challenge, it requires unnatural humility and perspective. In the wilderness denial is death. As Fears outlined, many people who are lost don't admit it to themselves until they are in a much worse situation.

For John Sain, the full weight of the moment became abundantly clear when he realized his leg was resting next to his rib cage. Sain's failure to admit his problem didn't begin when he broke his leg; it began when he failed to admit that he could be vulnerable in the wilderness in the first place. Relying on his lengthy experience and self-confidence, Sain didn't notify others of his location or bring a method of emergency communication. His overconfidence was the source of his predicament. The extreme pain Sain felt after trying and failing to stand, however, didn't allow him the luxury of denial.

Much like John Sain, Marvel, Inc., not only toyed with denial in the early 1990s, it wandered all the way to the edge of existence. The iconic comic book brand was at the peak of success in the early 1990s during the height of the comic book craze. Built through the 1960s, 1970s, and 1980s on a unique art style and compelling storytelling, the brand began to milk the market for everything it was worth.

Eyeing the potential to exploit passionate collectors in the comic book space, a businessman and investor named Phil Perelman purchased

Marvel in 1989 for $82.5 million.[9] Perelman immediately went on a spending spree, buying up comic book retailers and taking stakes in a toymaker, sticker company, and distribution company, ultimately investing upward of $700 million.[10]

Perelman then moved to raise prices and use gimmicks to encourage collectors to buy multiple copies of the same edition—gimmicks like releasing comic books with multiple covers and including exclusive trading cards in limited editions. The efforts worked, and Marvel began to make money hand over fist. But its very success created a sort of "market fatigue," and in just a few short years, collectors woke up to its implicit lie.

In a famous speech before thousands of comic book retailers in 1993, Neil Gaiman, writer of the Sandman series, told the group that their collective success was built on the misleading notion that the value of collectors' investments would continue to grow. He went on to compare the comic book craze to the infamous seventeenth-century tulip mania (generally recognized as the first modern market bubble), in which the value of tulip bulbs quickly rose to absurd levels, only to crash not long after.[11]

Gaiman's speech did not go over well, but it proved prescient. Between 1993 and 1996, comic books sales plummeted. The house of cards Phil Perelman built collapsed, and by 1996, Marvel filed for bankruptcy. As Scott Sassa, the company's chairman and CEO at the time, noted, "it was like everything that could go wrong did go wrong."

Marvel's denial didn't originate during its crisis. The decision to file for bankruptcy was a forced admission of its predicament. Marvel's denial arose as the company seeded the comic book bubble while gleefully neglecting its risks. After filing for bankruptcy, a tumultuous period ensued in which the company suffered under a protracted battle for control. Marvel finally emerged from bankruptcy with all-new leadership.

In a pivotal move by the board, Peter Cuneo was brought in as the new CEO. Cuneo was a seasoned executive whose list of accomplishments included multiple turnarounds at companies including Remington and Black & Decker.[12] One of his first moves was to instill a culture of honesty and forthrightness.

During Marvel's unexpected fall, a culture of fear had paralyzed employees, making them unwilling to admit weakness or vulnerability. This, obviously, made addressing internal problems difficult. Quoted in a *Forbes* article about the challenge, Cuneo said

> One of the changes was to make an atmosphere where it's okay to admit they have problems and challenges in [their] jobs. We can solve them together in 99% of the cases, but we need to know about them. What used to keep me up at night mostly was not problems I knew about, [but] other problems that I maybe didn't know about.[13]

As Cuneo instinctively knew, before you can navigate The Wild, you first must admit you're lost.

Submit to Reality

As John Sain stared at his unholstered pistol, he recognized the depth of his predicament. He was miles from the trail and had no water and barely any food. Every move was excruciating, and no one knew he was in trouble.

Before pulling the trigger, he decided to leave a note for his wife and children on his cell phone. Josh Dahlke documented Sain's note, in which he shared his love of watching his son play football and apologized for not being there anymore. He also encouraged his wife and daughter to continue to keep Jesus in their lives so that they could see each other again someday.[14] Sain saved the note in his phone, hoping that if his body were found, his last thoughts would be discovered and given to his family.

Sain's submission to his circumstances led him to a point of despair at the very moment when he needed cold reasoning and clear understanding of his situation to survive. The *U.S. Air Force Survival Manual (USAFSM)* calls this the "Crisis Period" and says it "is the point at which the person realizes the gravity of the situation and understands that the problem will not go away."[15]

Admitting you are lost is one thing; submitting to the things you can't control is another. The Wild has a way of humbling us. Much like the first time we lose sight of land on the open sea, stare into the vastness of a starry night, or see Earth from space, The Wild reminds us how small we truly are.

Most who face the reality of their lack of control simply freak out. The *USAFSM* says, "the response may be panic, behavior may be irrational, and judgment is impaired." This is because people instinctively allow the environment to control their actions.

Submitting to the reality of your circumstances is the first step to regaining internal control and recognizing that The Wild can never be governed. You are small. The Wild is big and overpowering. Survivors use this perspective to find clarity and then focus on the things that are within their control—first and foremost, their own minds.

The chief obstacle to this clarity is pride. J. Wayne Fears's survival book outlines a strange phenomenon in which lost people will actually hide from their rescuers due to the fear of shame and punishment. The young and old are especially susceptible to this challenge, but even the strongest outdoorsman in the prime of his life can fall victim to it.

We watched John Spillane experience the power of shame during the Perfect Storm in Chapter 1. As he and his helicopter crew were searching for a missing ship, they ran out of gas and abruptly found themselves in need of rescue. Spillane, a highly experienced para-jumper, bailed out of the crashing helicopter and was alone in the middle of the raging ocean, swallowing water and trying desperately to stay alive.

After an hour, he spotted two lights bobbing up and down in the waves. Initially elated, he began to swim toward his team. Then, suddenly, he found himself psychologically unable to move any closer. Believing that he likely wouldn't make it through the night, he decided it would be best to die alone. Sebastian Junger quotes Spillane as saying, "I didn't want them to see me go . . . I didn't want them to see me in pain."

Although Marvel's new CEO, Peter Cuneo, had a number of successful turnarounds under his belt, he knew the dangers of pride in crisis. In an interview with Neelima Mahajan at *Founding Fuel*, Cuneo said, "I'm always very careful to never think 'I've seen it all' because every situation is different and you have to be prepared. There are always new challenges and lessons. If you get smug or arrogant about your skills in this area, you're going to be in trouble."[16]

Cuneo's humility and submission to reality allowed him to recognize Marvel's dire situation for what it was. When he first came on board, Marvel had plans for a new trading card project, a Marvel-themed restaurant, and interactive CD-ROMs. But the company was cash poor, having only a few million dollars in the bank. Marvel was trying to make do with a meager 250 employees and endured a stock value of only 96 cents per share. All of these planned initiatives were designed to chase a market that didn't exist anymore. As Peter Sampson put it in an article for *Screen Crush*, "This was the kind of dated thinking that got Marvel into this mess."[17]

Marvel needed a new direction but could not get there without first submitting to reality. Pride kills in the wilderness. Brands that successfully navigate danger recognize themselves and their circumstances for what they really are.

Commit to Live

John Sain was angry. After he finished his note to his wife and kids, something awoke deep inside. He was mad at himself for even contemplating suicide, not to mention for getting into the situation in the first place. Sain holstered his pistol, placed his phone in a Ziploc bag, and told himself that he had to at least try.[18]

After you admit your challenge and submit to reality, your survival depends upon a very real but mysterious attitude known as the will to live. The *U.S. Air Force Survival Manual* defines the will to live as "the desire to live despite seemingly insurmountable ... obstacles."[19] The *USAFSM* says that the will to live occurs during the "Coping Period," a phase that begins "after the survivor recognizes the gravity of the situation and resolves to endure it rather than succumb."[20]

The will to live remains mysterious because, while it is documented as a vital part of survival, it's hard to nail down and define. Jim Collins famously noted a similar phenomenon that occurred during the Vietnam War in his book *Good to Great*. He asked Admiral James Stockdale, the highest-ranking POW at the time (who had his own harrowing survival story), which prisoners were the first to die in prison camps. Stockdale told him, "Oh, that's easy. The optimists." He went on to explain that the prisoners who pinned their hopes on getting out by an upcoming date were let down so often that they would eventually give up and die. This wasn't due to any physical ailment; it was simply because of their state of mind.[21]

The lack of a will to live is popularly called "give-up-itis." The term was coined during the Korean War to describe prisoners of war who died without explanation. They suffered from neither illness nor starvation; instead, they would literally will themselves to die. The *USAFSM* says the hopeless prisoners "withdrew themselves from the group, became despondent, then lay down and gave up."[22]

In one case of give-up-itis, a pilot flying over the Canadian wilderness had to land an airplane in the middle of a lake due to engine trouble. After landing without injury, he exited the airplane as it bobbed in the water and spotted a shoreline roughly two hundred yards in the distance. He began swimming toward the shoreline but inexplicably returned to the aircraft, smoked a cigar, and committed suicide. A rescue crew arrived less than twenty-four hours later and found him dead.

The profound truth is that, in many circumstances, regardless of training or resources, survival comes down to a choice. Stories of hope and heroism are just as prevalent as those that end in despair. The difference is in the will.

In 1999, Marvel's new CEO committed the company to live. Suffering under $250 million in debt after the bankruptcy, Marvel needed cash. Peter Cuneo's first move was to pursue an aggressive licensing model that included film, television, and consumer products. The decision immediately ramped up short-term brand awareness and brought in much-needed cash. Cuneo then outsourced the in-house development of role-playing games and action figures to free up capital.[23]

Next, he focused on fostering a culture that could believe in itself again. Coming out of bankruptcy, Marvel faced ailing internal health. Cuneo emphasized honesty and consistency to regain trust. Reflecting on the turnaround, he said,

> If you want to establish a new culture, back it up with actions. Talk is very simple, but most employees will not believe you until they see you behaving in a way that suggests that you really will act on the things you're saying.

After solving Marvel's short-term cash needs, Cuneo sought growth by fostering relationships with multiple film and video game development companies to enable quicker production and distribution and attract partners who were passionate about individual Marvel characters. He said he believes his greatest breakthrough was investing in comic book development instead of abandoning it. During the 1990s, Marvel's reputation suffered due to declining quality. Cuneo moved to change that by viewing comic book development as an investment in R&D as much as a potential revenue source. But first he had to quash a culture that punished failure. Commenting on Marvel's innovation problem, Cuneo said that you have to "tell people it's okay to fail . . . you will have failures, and that's okay. But [employees] won't believe you until you back it up."

To improve quality, Cuneo issued a mandate that mediocrity would no longer be endured, and he recruited top talent, an area long neglected by the company. Marvel then shortened story arcs and pursued additional distribution partners to attract new readers. The initiatives would lead to double-digit market share gains.

What seems in retrospect like a series of savvy business decisions was viewed as anything but during the hard turnaround years. That's because fostering the will to live isn't easy. Reflecting on the decade-long turnaround, Cuneo commented in a *Forbes* interview that "It's not romantic. It's romantic after the case." He went on to say, "When you're in a turnaround every day, people are unhappy, and people are unhappy with you every day even if they don't know you because you represent change."[24]

After its initial success in film licensing, Marvel used the learnings it gained from working with some of Hollywood's top studios to bring production in house. In 2005, the company put up its top intellectual property as collateral to gain the funding it needed to create Marvel Studios. A string of smash hits followed at the box office, and by 2009 Marvel was sold to Disney for $4.5 billion.

An Unexpected Journey

John Sain's broken leg flopped behind him like a flag in the wind. After saying several prayers, he used every ounce of will to begin crawling. He could hear the bones in his leg grinding as he fought for every desperate inch. Then he fell.

While trying to cross a tangled mess of logs and brush, Sain slipped off the side and smashed into the ground. The impact snapped both his leg bones back into place, giving him the opportunity to apply a makeshift leg splint.

He started scooting his way through trees and underbrush. The process was enormously painful and tedious, and his knuckles bled from abuse. His goal was to find the trail before the weekend ended. As the sun began to fall, he made a small campfire and tried to sleep under a survival blanket.

The next morning he resumed inching his way toward the trail. Dehydration was setting in. Sain tried to eat some peanuts, but his mouth was so dry he choked. After eleven grueling hours, he was exhausted and in extreme pain.

More than once, circumstances raised his hopes. At one point, Sain spotted a firefighting helicopter flying overhead; he tried creating signal fires and shooting SOS shots into the air but couldn't get the chopper's attention. With the sun again setting, Sain knew his time was running out. He could only go so long without water, and his strength was about to give out.

He decided to crawl through the coming darkness and try to reach the area where he believed the firefighters might be. In the middle of the night, Sain fell upon a small creek that provided his first taste of water in nearly two days. Soaking wet, he dragged himself out of the creek and made a small fire to endure the rest of the painful night.

As the morning of the third day approached, Sain finally made his way back to the trail. Suffering complete fatigue, he lay there, immobilized, and began praying. He didn't have the strength to go another inch. Josh Dahlke, writing for *Outdoor Life*, documented Sain's final prayer that Sunday morning: "I said, 'Lord, I'm not going to make it another day. I need help. I need you to bring somebody to this trail.' "[25]

Less than thirty minutes later, the sound of a motorcycle reverberated through the trees. Within hours, Sain would be in a hospital bed, surrounded by friends and family, grateful to be alive.

John Sain's story almost ended much differently. As the horror of his injury and predicament became clear, he considered the unthinkable. But as he contemplated such an end and wrote his last thoughts to his family, something powerful awoke deep inside: his will to live.

As you face The Wild, your talent and resources are important, but none of those matter if you don't have the right mindset. Giving in to a blind instinct for action may take you down an even darker path. First, stop. Your act must be inaction. Do nothing. Force yourself to be still.

Through humility and the clarity it provides you, you'll have the opportunity to admit that you are lost, submit to the reality of your circumstances, and commit to live.

The *U.S. Air Force Survival Manual* encourages us that "With the proper attitude, almost anything is possible."[26] In the end, the will to live is a question of whether you believe survival is worth the effort. John Sain and innumerable others have proven that the proper mindset can help us overcome nearly any obstacle, no matter how impossible it seems. So don't waste time worrying if your brand has what it takes to survive. It likely does if you believe it's worth it.

Survival Tips for Practical Application

Humans are capable of near miracles when they put their minds to it. With the right attitude, you can navigate anything The Wild throws at you.

Keep in Mind

- Survival experts everywhere train people who are lost to S.T.O.P.: sit, think, observe, plan.
- People who navigate The Wild admit that they are lost, submit to the circumstances, and commit to live.
- The will to live is a mysterious but powerful attitude shared among all who survive.

Survival Tips

To navigate The Wild:

- Outline your blind spots. Is your brand in denial?
- Beware the blinding power of hubris. If you don't seek humility, The Wild will do it for you.
- Cultivate your brand's will to live by staying positive and asking the most important question: Are you worth it?

Notes

1. John 'Lofty' Wiseman, *SAS Survival Handbook: The Ultimate Guide to Surviving Anywhere*, 3rd ed. (New York: William Morrow, 2014), 10.
2. Josh Dahlke, "One Wrong Step," *Outdoor Life*, April 2016, 41.
3. J. Wayne Fears, *The Pocket Outdoor Survival Guide: The Ultimate Guide for Short-Term Survival* (New York: Skyhorse, 2011), 113.
4. Fears, *The Pocket Outdoor Survival Guide*, 113–115.
5. Fears, *The Pocket Outdoor Survival Guide*, 44.
6. Dahlke, "One Wrong Step," 39.
7. *Merriam- Webster*, s.v. "Courage," accessed September 1, 2016, http://www.merriam-webster.com/dictionary/courage.
8. *Oxford Dictionary*, s.v. "Courage," accessed August 3, 2016, http://www.oxforddictionaries.com/us/definition/american_english/courage.
9. Ryan Lambie, "How Marvel Went from Bankruptcy to Billions," *DenOfGeek.com*, February 13, 2015, http://www.denofgeek.com/movies/marvel/34092/how-marvel-went-from-bankruptcy-to-billions.
10. Lambie, "How Marvel Went from Bankruptcy to Billions."
11. Lambie, "How Marvel Went from Bankruptcy to Billions."
12. Robert Reiss, "How Marvel Became a Business Superhero," *Forbes*, February 1, 2010, http://www.forbes.com/2010/02/01/peter-cuneo-marvel-leadership-managing-turnaround.html.
13. Neelima Mahajan, "Peter Cuneo, Turnaround Superhero," *Founding Fuel*, April 8, 2015, http://www.foundingfuel.com/article/peter-cuneo-turnaround-superhero/.
14. Dahlke, "One Wrong Step," 41.
15. *U.S. Air Force Survival Manual*, 51.
16. Mahajan, "Peter Cuneo, Turnaround Superhero."
17. Mike Sampson, "How Marvel Risked Everything to Go from Bankruptcy to Billions," *ScreenCrush.com*, April 23, 2015, http://screencrush.com/marvel-bankruptcy-billions/?trackback=tsmclip.
18. Dahlke, "One Wrong Step," 41.
19. *U.S. Air Force Survival Manual AFR*, 64–4; *Search and Rescue Survival Training*, Vol. 1, PDF, Washington, DC: Department of the Air Force, 51, https://docs.google.com/file/d/0BwBVZQFLg8OfcHdnNHpTUmdMRjg/edit.
20. *U.S. Air Force Survival Manual*, 52.

21. Jim Collins, *Good to Great: Why Some Companies Make the Leap . . . and Others Don't* (New York: Harper Business, 2001), 185.
22. *U.S. Air Force Survival Manual*, 50.
23. Reiss, "How Marvel Became a Business Superhero."
24. Mahajan, "Peter Cuneo, Turnaround Superhero."
25. Dahlke, "One Wrong Step," 43.
26. *U.S. Air Force Survival Manual*, 52.

CHAPTER 7

Orient

Shackleton and five others . . . set off through the Drake Passage—a name to bring dread even to seasoned mariners—in the almost impossible hope of making landfall on South Georgia, eight hundred miles away, and summoning help from the whaling stations there.[1]

—The James Caird Society

Five hundred and six days into a disastrous attempt to be the first humans to traverse Antarctica, Ernest Shackleton and his crew of marooned sailors teetered on the brink of survival. After enduring the most inhospitable terrain on earth, the loss of their ship to the violent crush of converging ice fields, and two failed attempts to march across the frozen wasteland to safety, Shackleton knew they must take action or accept certain death.

Faced with no good options, Shackleton made the desperate decision to set sail for an island 800 miles away with a handful of his men in a twenty-foot makeshift lifeboat through the most perilous waters on earth. Even if the crew could survive subzero temperatures, quickly diminishing rations, and hypothermia, they had to find their way to South Georgia with hastily repaired navigation tools and near-zero visibility, using what Shackleton called "dead reckoning" most of the way. And there was no room for error. If the crew's navigation was off by less than a degree, they would be swept past the island by the fast-moving current and lost at sea. Thus, the sailors held their fates and those of the rest of their marooned crewmates in their numb, shaking hands.[2]

How could Shackleton ever hope to survive a voyage that could be described as something just short of flying from earth to the moon in a Boeing 747 with a crew of astronauts clinging to life and only a pretty good guess for where the moon might be?

Having fostered your will to live, orienting yourself is the next step to navigating The Wild. This fact is brought eerily to life by Randy Gallistel, a cognitive neuroscientist at Rutgers University in New Jersey, who says that most dead hikers are found within a mile or less of where they were lost.[3]

While any good survivalist will recommend always staying put when lost, most people will instinctively try to find their way to safety despite the fact that their chances of walking in circles are surprisingly high.

The theory that lost people walk in circles was put to the test by research conducted by the Max Planck Institute for Biological Cybernetics. The Institute's study entailed dropping hikers into the middle of forests in Germany and the Sahara desert; the hikers were then told to do their best to walk in a straight line. GPS was used to track the hikers' movement.

According to a story about the study published by *Current Biology*, "no matter how hard people tried to walk in a straight line, they often ended up going in circles without ever realizing that they were crossing their own paths."[4]

In a follow-up study, the hikers were blindfolded to remove visual cues, resulting in them "going in surprisingly small circles—with a diameter of less than 66 feet."[5] The biggest difference between the hikers who walked in a straight line and those who walked in circles was the visibility of environmental cues like the sun or the moon. Emily Sohn at Discovery.com went on to say that hikers walked in circles in overcast conditions or at night after the moon had set, confirming that "without landmarks to guide us, people really do go around and around."[6]

But the biggest threat of all may be less that the lost are prone to walk in circles and more that, lacking bearings, the body may not obey the brain's commands. Ominously, the circles walked by the subjects in these studies weren't due to some giant blunder or miscalculation. Instead, Jan Souman, a psychologist at the Max Planck Institute, hypothesized in a *Live Science* article that "With every step, a small deviation is likely added to a person's cognitive sense of what's straight, and these deviations accumulate to send that individual veering around in ever tighter circles as time goes on."[7]

Souman's findings leave us with the disquieting notion that, although we may have exceptionally good intentions, our bodies will undermine our minds as thousands of "deviations" add up to an existential mistake. "Just walking in a straight line seems like such a simple and natural thing to do," says Souman, "but if you think about it, it's quite [a] complicated thing going on in the brain."[8]

The research raises the frightening prospect that even if you have the best of intentions for your lost brand, your actions may not align with your purpose. Without clear market cues, brands lose their bearings. And without bearings, brands drift.

A case in point is Apple's crisis leading up to Steve Jobs's return in 1997. The brand's implosion represents a classic example of a company losing its bearings and walking in circles. But few have noted the masterful use of everyday survival skills Jobs employed to navigate the company back toward success.

Much like Shackleton's view when facing the impassable Drake Passage, Apple's prospect of survival couldn't have looked worse in the mid-1990s. Under the leadership of a revolving door of CEOs, Apple's product line proliferated as it took a shotgun approach to market success. Speaking to this product multiplicity, Benj Edwards wrote in a *Macworld* article of a "dizzying array" of products and product variations, "few of which made a profit."[9]

Facing impending bankruptcy, Apple was losing money like water through a sieve. It endured annual losses of more than $1 billion and shrinking market share. And behind closed doors, multiple board members attempted to sell the company, to no avail.[10]

Apple had lost its way. With no idea where the brand fit in the world, it drifted from trend to trend, chasing the wind and short-term success. And if Jobs hadn't intervened when he did, Apple would be just another dead brand found within a mile of where it was lost.

How to Find Your Bearings

Many attribute the success of leaders like Jobs and Shackleton to some innate genius, out of reach for the average person. While the methods used by these storied leaders require years of experience and a penchant for decisiveness, they reflect more a masterful use of survival skills than superhuman ability.

Navigating ambiguous environments requires the very qualities that do not come naturally in extreme situations: patient observation and uncommon discipline. Survival experts recommend a variety of methods to orient yourself and navigate difficult terrain.[11] These methods can be summed up in three steps:

1. Read the signs.
2. Build a map.
3. Focus on short-term goals.

1. Read the Signs

In the wilderness, clues to help you establish your bearings are everywhere. Hidden in birds' nests. Staring at you in the sky. Rustling along a river. Even the wind and the plants speak volumes. While most people who are lost in the wilderness have little to no knowledge of the plethora of information around them, the shrewd outdoorsman knows how to read the signs.

As Gallistel explained on Discovery.com, "to counter the tendency to spiral . . . hikers [should] learn some simple Boy Scout tricks. Moss grows on the north side of trees. There is less vegetation on the south-facing side of a valley than on its north-facing slopes. And the sun moves from east to west throughout the day."[12]

In extreme terrain, the industrious survivor doesn't just rely on GPS or a compass but knows how to read the very earth itself. Shadows can be used to divine direction and time of day. Flora and fauna grow most profusely toward the sun. Tree bark will have a tighter grain on the north side of the trunk. And tree rings will be more widely spaced on the side that faces the equator.[13] The information you need is there if you choose to observe it.

Steve Jobs wisely read the signs when he took the reins of Apple in 1997. As entrenched competitors created a paralyzing web of partnerships in hardware and retail, Jobs planned to use the only advantage at Apple's disposal: agility. While competitors fought for the status quo, Jobs understood that the future belonged to an entirely new paradigm of communication and personal computing devices that current industry power players were ill equipped to create.[14]

It didn't take prescience to make this assessment, but clear-eyed, sober judgment built on years of patient observation. The same type of subtle clues that help you orient yourself in the wilderness also surround your brand every day. They are found in the world around you, in your performance numbers, on your team's faces, and even in the subliminal recesses of your mind. If you are like most, you miss the clues as they float by in a sea of data. But if you have the uncommon patience and discipline required to train yourself to read the brand signs, the benefits are incalculable.

The surest method to read the brand signs is to listen to the market. Careful observation, customer interviews, trend reports, and market research can all help if you are willing to listen. Capturing the information is the first and simplest step. But don't give in to the temptation to stop there. The real value of any information is in its interpretation. The

extent to which you put the information to use through rigorous interpretation, seeking insights, and questioning the data and your bias is the
extent to which you can act on the information you have gathered.

Jobs didn't arrive at his spot-on reckoning of the PC market in the mid
1990s because he had access to hidden information. In fact, all of Jobs's
information was just as available to competitors as it was to him. Instead,
Jobs gathered the facts, removed his bias as best he could, and made a
logical deduction as to where they would lead. And most importantly, he
used the perspective he gained through his absence from Apple to see the
market conditions clearly.

Shackleton's "reading of the market" before the voyage to South
Georgia was also based on sober judgment and careful observation.
Understanding that rescuers were not likely to arrive, Shackleton had
three options: attempt a third and likely fatal march through the Antarctic
wasteland, make the perilous journey to South Georgia, where whaling
stations were sure to be manned and stocked with rations, or make sail
for a closer and safer island, fighting the prevailing winds in a makeshift
lifeboat. Understanding the risks, Shackleton didn't choose the closest or
most immediate option but the one that gave his crew the best chance to
survive.

Internal performance measures are also a key method of reading the
signs. Your team's alignment is one of the strongest indicators of whether
your brand has its bearings. A team that has achieved Noble Equilibrium
is tightly aligned around vision, mission, values, and objectives. It knows
exactly where it is and where it is going, has little internal politics, and
has employees who share a common understanding of the brand.

In the wilderness, a common mistake made by even the most seasoned
survivalist is overestimating performance or imbuing negative facts with
illogical hope. As John Wiseman noted in *The SAS Survival Handbook*,
"One of the most common errors people make is to overestimate how
much ground they have covered. It is usually much less. One way around
this is to fit the ground where you are to the map, rather than the map to
where you think you are."[15]

Fitting the "map to where you think you are" is a dangerous but recurrent blunder that involves suiting the facts to your intentions rather than letting them speak for themselves. And it most often occurs at the worst possible time: when your brand begins to drift.

Often overlooked, another important sign to read is your gut. Your gut isn't always right, but if you learn to decipher its mixed signals, it can often point you in the right direction. When you are considering an important brand decision, for instance, fear can often indicate which direction is bolder and, therefore, likely to have a bigger market impact. A team's natural propensity, however, is to seek safety and convenience. But in today's economy, where disruption is the rule, an unhealthy aversion to risk can actually increase your chances of drifting.

Fear is the most common emotion in the wilderness. When honed and focused, it can be productive. But it is also often the source of our worst decisions. The right thing to do in harsh circumstances usually isn't the easy thing to do. Fear, discomfort, and anxiety should be accepted as potential positive reactions when considering any potential plan. Without them, your plan of action may not be aggressive enough.

2. Build a Map

In *The SAS Survival Handbook*, Wiseman recommends building a map to fill in gaps in knowledge, writing, "The survivor may not be lucky enough to have a map and should then set about making one."[16] As you read the signs and begin orienting yourself, your immediate next step is to build a map of your surroundings. You can think of your map as the foundation for your plan. Your brand map can take many forms, including a market analysis, internal audit, or, in some circumstances, even a literal map. All of the intel you have gathered should be codified and noted, with key areas of interest, danger zones, rough terrain, and regions of opportunity outlined.

When Steve Jobs took the reins in 1997, Apple was months away from bankruptcy. As Jobs built Apple's "brand map," he was most interested in finding basic survival necessities in the form of an infusion of cash. He knew that any additional work would be in vain should the company be unable to survive. In a move that stunned the industry and Apple employees alike, Jobs announced that Microsoft would invest $150 million in Apple with a commitment to develop Microsoft Office software for the Macintosh.[17]

While painful for many at Apple, the deal, as Brad Stone described, was "a cold calculation by Jobs that Apple did not need to win the old battle for the PC in order to prevail in a dawning war for digital media devices and the Internet."[18] The move would, over time, prove that Jobs had masterfully read the signs and built an accurate map of the market conditions.

According to Wiseman, to build an adequate map, one must "find the best vantage point and look out over the terrain. Climbing a tree may give a better view."[19] Perspective is vital in map building. As you work to build your brand map, seek every opportunity to "climb a tree" to get a better view of the lay of the land.

The day before Shackleton's attempt to sail through the Drake Passage, he noted how he and two crew members "climbed to the summit of the seaward rocks and examined the ice from a better vantage point than the beach offered."[20] After setting sail the next day, the additional perspective ended up saving the crew's lives, as they were forced to unexpectedly change course "to avoid the great lumps of ice that were flung about in the heave of the sea." The crew narrowly escaped by "running . . . towards a gap [Shackleton] had seen in the morning from the high ground."[21]

Perspective is difficult for a team to achieve internally, as it faces a multitude of pressures that lead to bias, self-deception, and Savage Equilibrium. These pressures can include a natural drive for self-preservation, internal politics, turf wars, and disloyalty, all of which undermine efforts to build an accurate map. A tried-and-true method of gaining perspective is hiring it. While consultants have a bad reputation for borrowing your watch to tell you what time it is, their fundamental value is their distance from your problem. A clear mind and fresh eyes are priceless in the wilderness, and if you need to hire someone to climb the tree for you, do not hesitate.

If you do not have the resources or ability to incorporate the perspective of an outsider, you must begin the difficult journey of climbing the tree yourself. Your main obstacles will be your closeness to the situation, your emotional attachment to the brand, and your ability to deal with internal conflict. The degree to which you can separate yourself, judge with clear eyes, and act on your observations will determine how high you can ascend. It isn't impossible, but it is difficult, and uncommon discipline is required to succeed.

Wiseman goes on to recommend that survivors "Make a general map with blank patches and then fill them in as you gain more information from other vantage points and from your explorations."[22] Climbing a tree is important but can only fill in so much of the blank area on your map. When facing unknown territory, it is essential that you send out scouting parties to document what lies ahead and report the findings.

Many marketers interpret "scouting" simply as pretesting creative, which can wield unscientific and unhelpful, if not dangerous, results. Instead, focus on tried-and-true scouting methods like competitive analysis, field testing, and research that focuses on observation and real-world experimentation.

Competitive analysis should be your first scouting effort and can reveal as much about what you shouldn't do as what you should do. It is a vital method for orienting yourself and filling in your brand map and can take a variety of forms, such as secret shopping, comparative brand studies, and multiple methods of secondary research like industry positioning and marketing reviews.

Jobs's turnaround efforts at Apple were rooted in a competitive analysis that suggested what competitors *wouldn't* do. Recognizing that competitors' internal incentives were tied to sustaining the status quo, Jobs made previously unthinkable alliances and then focused on trailblazing territory where he knew competitors wouldn't go.

A simple method of competitive analysis my firm employs is called the Wall Test. To conduct the Wall Test, gather every bit of competitive marketing materials you can find, including advertising, collateral, logos, taglines, and even printouts of competitors' websites and social media presence. Then cover the walls with it. When you see it all in one place, industry conventions will immediately jump out at you, including overused colors, design clichés, common language, and more. Use this information to identify where your competitors are congregating so you have a better idea of how different your brand really is. If you place your brand on the wall and it blends in with competitors, you have failed the Wall Test.

In addition to competitive analysis, field testing can be invaluable in the brand wilderness. While testing advertising creative materials in artificial conditions can open up a rabbit hole of unscientific gobbledygook, field testing your messaging and products is the gold standard of intel gathering. In an uncertain environment, piloting new messaging and products in structured, real-world scenarios allows you to gain valuable, actionable intelligence without taking on the risk and cost of marketwide rollouts.

The packaged goods industry, led by Procter & Gamble, has employed this method to great success for many years by selecting test-market geographies, scaling budgets and timelines accordingly, and setting up key metrics and surrounding pilots with marketing support. Results are then reviewed, and products or programs may be tweaked and retested before being expanded nationwide. In today's digital world, where targeting can be done not only by geography but by demographics, behavior, interests, or a host of other options, this is easier to do than ever.

Some brands are even using social media to test product interest before embarking on expensive bricks-and-mortar expansions. Stuart Weitzman, a high-end shoe company interested in international expansion, used Facebook to test product interest in countries around the world. Writing for *AdWeek*, Jeffery Lafferty noted that the company tested its popularity in potential markets using relatively inexpensive Facebook advertising, "then expanded their presence in countries where the Facebook metrics were more positive."[23] The company used the intel to expand into countries it may not have anticipated offering immediate opportunity, including Dubai and Mexico, among others.

While most premier brands understand that research is the lifeblood of product development, few apply the model to their marketing efforts. Applying the R&D model to marketing requires a shift in thinking, but it can reap hefty rewards.

General Electric has embraced marketing R&D with both arms, pioneering new models in digital media, content marketing, and brand publishing. Ted Mann documented GE's approach in the *Wall Street Journal*, saying, "GE has been exploring the changing media landscape aggressively and early, taking the decline of traditional print media as an opening to try new ways to reach young, influential audiences." He wrote that GE is "a surprising and noteworthy experimenter with new media" and is investing "some 40% of the company's [marketing] spending"[24] on innovative new marketing models.

While a 40 percent investment is far too aggressive for most brands, we recommend that our clients set aside 5 to 10 percent of their marketing budgets for experimentation and risk taking. This approach not only encourages innovation but, more importantly, gives team members structured permission to fail—a key requirement when exploring unknown territory and building your brand map.

3. Focus on Short-Term Goals

The final step required to establish and retain your bearings is to focus your energy on achieving short-term goals within the context of your brand's long-term objective. The process seems simple enough but is under constant assault by impatience, distraction, and changing circumstances.

Shackleton's violent voyage in the midst of Drake Passage demanded short-term attention. Enduring an experience in which "every surge of the sea was an enemy to be watched and circumvented," the crew managed dwindling supplies, treated frostbite, and desperately kept watch for any sign of the sun. Shackleton described the ordeal by saying, "our thoughts did not embrace much more than the necessities of the hour."[25]

In *Leading from the Edge*, leadership expert Dennis Perkins calls these short-term goals "quick victories" and says, "while pursuing this long-term target, leaders also must be vigilant in focusing the scarce resources of the organization on critical short-term tasks that create momentum and ensure survival."[26]

Paradoxically, the key to retaining your bearings is to use the Bearings Cycle™, a continual process that includes determining a landmark, piling stones along the way, then confirming you made it. In a bit of irony, the best way to walk in a straight line is to engage in a never-ending cycle.

Following the Bearings Cycle is the difference between progress and brand drift, but it requires unusual amounts of tenacity and discipline. Jobs

The Bearings Cycle

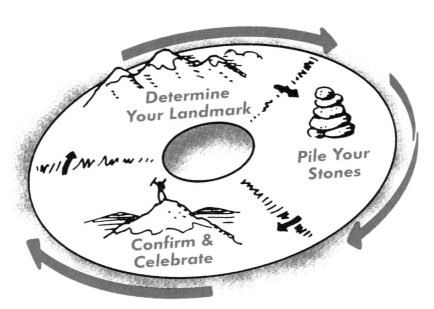

Figure 7.1   *The Bearings Cycle*

acted swiftly to establish Apple's version of the Bearings Cycle by determining the company's first landmark: draconian focus on product development. Writing on the topic, Brad Stone noted in *Bloomberg Business* that "what Apple removed from technology products, Jobs liked to say, was just as important as what it added. He banished elements like separate numerical keypads, floppy disk drives, and computer mice with two buttons."[27]

Benj Edwards further noted in *Macworld* that "ultimately, Jobs axed more than 70 percent of Apple's hardware and software products," including laying off more than three thousand employees in his first year back alone.[28]

With tenacity and discipline as your foundation, set out to initiate your own Bearings Cycle. Determining your landmark is just as much about what you choose to focus on as what you don't. Your landmark should be on the path toward your ultimate goal yet be in your line of sight and near enough to be readily achievable. But be warned: your first temptation will be to select more than one landmark. Multiple landmarks will only result in dividing your team's time and attention and ultimately splitting up the group. As Shackleton's navigator, Frank Worsley, observed, "Shackleton was always opposed to splitting the party, and he very wisely refused to consider such a move . . . although the temptation to explore . . . was almost overwhelming."[29]

In a business environment, if your overarching goal is to increase sales, your first landmark might be to improve sales team hiring practices, outsource sales functions, or better equip the sales team with marketing support. Whatever the case, select one landmark and focus on that until you have achieved it, then move on to the next.

After determining your landmark, "pile your stones" to create a sense of progress and protect yourself from veering off course. Moving toward your landmark is perhaps the most difficult step in the Bearings Cycle, as impatience and distraction tempt the team to make decisions that result in brand drift. Wiseman writes that your best method of protection is to "look back frequently," and "set up sticks or piles of stones in alignment with each other so that you can check that you are not deviating from your route."[30]

The building of stone piles, known as cairns, is an ancient practice that is found in nearly every culture around the world. According to a historical review of the custom by Michael Gaige on Outdoors.org, cairns were used by the early Norse and Vikings, and you can find them across the Tibetan Plateau, the Mongolian Steppe, and throughout the Inca road system.[31]

The custom is used for both practical and emotional purposes, marking trails and encouraging fellow journeyers that "someone has been here before." Gaige goes on to note that cairns were "erected for navigation, spiritual offering, or as monuments of remembrance."

As you pile your own stones, remember that your purpose is to continually review performance in an effort to create a feeling of progress, avoid repeating mistakes, and identify unexpected obstacles so you can adjust accordingly. As you keep your eye on your landmark, take time to gauge ongoing success to keep your team's spirits high and ensure you're walking in a straight line.

Once you've arrived at your landmark, make a point of publicly confirming and celebrating the completion of your Bearings Cycle. This gives the team a chance to enjoy a small win and gather its strength before turning its attention toward restarting the Bearings Cycle and determining the next landmark.

In the polar south, where long stretches of darkness take an unusual mental and physical toll, Ernest Shackleton wrote about his habit of using any excuse to celebrate, including "a concert in the evening" that created "a scene of noisy merriment in strange contrast with the cold, silent world that lay outside."[32]

Writing on the topic, Dennis Perkins noted in *Leading from the Edge* that "under survival conditions, laughter is an unnatural act . . . yet, under extreme pressure, the ability to lighten up . . . can break a spiral of depression and stimulate creativity."[33]

In the midst of the wilderness, it can be tempting to overlook celebration. But the importance of encouraging the team to release pent-up energy and emotion can't be overstated. The journey is hard, and marking

a thousand small victories along the way is far more important than waiting, sometimes forever, for the "big win."

The Voyage of the *James Caird*

On day 506 of Shackleton's expedition, the six-person crew of the lifeboat named the *James Caird* set out on the 800-mile journey to South
Georgia. Soaked to the skin by the Antarctic waters, the sailors took
one-minute shifts chipping the ever-growing ice from the deck of their
continually sinking ship. Early in the voyage, the compass was broken
by harsh conditions, forcing a hasty repair using adhesive tape from their
medical chest. And at night, the steersman could not use the compass for
fear of running out of matches.

Over the next seventeen days, enduring starvation, malnutrition,
and hypothermia, the crew saw the sun just four times. During those
moments, crew members risked their lives to orient themselves by hanging from the mainmast with one arm to catch a brief glimpse of the sun
and snap a reading at the crest of each massive wave.

Hours away from death, the crew captured their bearings from one of
those rare sightings of the sun and knew they were just a hundred miles
from South Georgia. Being experienced sailors, they knew when they
spotted a bit of kelp that they were inching closer to land. Later, they
spotted two shag birds sitting on a mass of kelp, and, in the words of
Shackleton, "[We] knew then that we must be within ten or fifteen miles
of the shore. These birds are as sure an indication of the proximity of land
as a lighthouse is, for they never venture far to sea."[34]

After several harrowing attempts to land on the inhospitable shores
of South Georgia, Shackleton and the crew of the *James Caird* finally
made landfall, saving their own lives, and, ultimately, the lives of their
marooned brothers 800 miles away.

Much like Jobs's unlikely turnaround of ailing Apple, the voyage of
the *James Caird* was supposed to be impossible. The ambiguity of The

Wild can make survival seem unthinkable, and the ability of leaders like Jobs and Shackleton to navigate uncertainty is often regarded as beyond an average person's reach. But if you understand the principles at work in the wilderness, you can navigate any circumstance with the same confidence and mastery as these great leaders.

By appreciating your brand's natural propensity to "walk in circles," you can counteract it with uncommon tenacity and discipline. Then you can learn to read the signs, build a map, and focus on short-term goals, allowing you to find and keep your brand's bearings in the wilderness.

Survival Tips for Practical Application

Whether your brand is completely lost or only drifting off course, orienting yourself is an important step in your march toward success.

Keep in Mind

- When navigating The Wild, finding your bearings means the difference between life and death.
- Your chances of walking in circles when lost are surprisingly high.
- In the absence of bearings, your brain and your body may work toward different ends.

Survival Tips

To navigate The Wild:

- Read the brand signs by observing the market, keeping an eye on performance measures, engaging your team, and listening to your gut.
- Build your brand map by "climbing a tree" for perspective and scouting unknown territory through competitive analysis, field testing, and investing in marketing R&D.

- Focus on short-term goals and avoid brand drift by implementing the Bearings Cycle to determine your landmark, pile your stones, and confirm and celebrate.

Notes

1. "Voyage of James Caird," *James Caird Society*, accessed September 1, 2016, http://www.jamescairdsociety.com/the-james-caird/voyage-of-james-caird/.
2. Ernest Shackleton, *South: The Endurance Expedition* (New York: Signet, 1999), 188–195.
3. Discovery Communications, "People Naturally Walk in Circles," *Seeker. com*, August 19, 2009, http://www.seeker.com/people-naturally-walk-in-circles-1764713193.html#news.discovery.com.
4. Discovery Communications, "People Naturally Walk in Circles."
5. Discovery Communications, "People Naturally Walk in Circles."
6. Emily Sohn, "Turns Out, Lost People Really Do Walk in Circles: Without Landmarks as Guides, You'll Need a Compass or GPS When Outdoors," *NBCNews.com*, August 20, 2009, http://www.nbcnews.com/id/32494981/ns/technology_and_science-science/t/turns-out-lost-people-really-do-walk-circles/#.V5E2G5OAOko.
7. Natalie Wolchover, "Why Do Humans Walk in Circles?" *Livescience.com*, August 5, 2011, http://www.livescience.com/33431-why-humans-walk-circles.html.
8. Discovery Communications, "People Naturally Walk in Circles."
9. Benj Edwards, "Steve Jobs's Seven Key Decisions," *Macworld.com*, September 2012, http://www.macworld.com/article/2009941/steve-jobss-seven-key-decisions.html.
10. Brad Stone, "Steve Jobs: The Return, 1997–2011," *Bloomber.com*, accessed August 20, 2016, http://www.bloomberg.com/news/articles/2011-10-06/steve-jobs-the-return-1997-2011.
11. John 'Lofty' Wiseman, *SAS Survival Handbook: The Ultimate Guide to Surviving Anywhere*, 3rd ed. (New York: William Morrow, 2014), 348–371.
12. Emily Sohn, "Turns Out, Lost People Really Do Walk in Circles: Without Landmarks as Guides, You'll Need a Compass or GPS When Outdoors."

13. Wiseman, *SAS Survival Handbook: The Ultimate Guide to Surviving Anywhere*, 359.

14. Stone, "Steve Jobs: The Return, 1997–2011."

15. Wiseman, *SAS Survival Handbook: The Ultimate Guide to Surviving Anywhere*, 355.

16. Wiseman, *SAS Survival Handbook: The Ultimate Guide to Surviving Anywhere*, 355.

17. Stone, "Steve Jobs: The Return, 1997–2011."

18. Stone, "Steve Jobs: The Return, 1997–2011."

19. Wiseman, *SAS Survival Handbook: The Ultimate Guide to Surviving Anywhere*, 355.

20. Shackleton, *South: The Endurance Expedition*, 178.

21. Shackleton, *South: The Endurance Expedition*, 181.

22. Wiseman, *SAS Survival Handbook: The Ultimate Guide to Surviving Anywhere*, 355.

23. Justin Lafferty, "Case Study: How Stuart Weitzman Used Facebook to Test International Markets," *Social Times*, July 29, 2013, http://www.adweek.com/socialtimes/case-study-how-stuart-weitzman-used-facebook-to-test-international-markets/295130.

24. Ted Mann, "GE Touts Its New-Media Cred: 122-Year-Old Company Embraces BuzzFeed, Pinterest, Tumblr," *The Wall Street Journal*, December 1, 2014, http://www.wsj.com/articles/ge-touts-its-new-media-cred-1417482888.

25. Shackleton, *South: The Endurance Expedition*, 189.

26. Dennis N. T. Perkins, *Leading at the Edge: Leadership Lessons from the Extraordinary Saga of Shackleton's Antarctic Expedition* (New York: Amacom, 2000), 15.

27. Stone, "Steve Jobs: The Return, 1997–2011."

28. Edwards, "Steve Jobs's Seven Key Decisions,"

29. Perkins, *Leading at the Edge*, 70.

30. Wiseman, *SAS Survival Handbook: The Ultimate Guide to Surviving Anywhere*, 379.

31. Michael Gaige, "A Natural and Social History of Cairn Building and Maintenance," *AMC Outdoors*, February 28, 2013, http://www.outdoors.org/articles/amc-outdoors/cairns-history-building-maintenance/.

32. Shackleton, *South: The Endurance Expedition*, 52.

33. Perkins, *Leading at the Edge*, 113.

34. Shackleton, *South: The Endurance Expedition*, 195.

CHAPTER 8

FOCUS

*To escape: that was the obsession of the new optimists . . . to the west
there was a solid wall of towering mountains, but this did not deter Parrado. No sooner had he learned of the cancellation of the search than
he announced his intention of setting off—on his own, if necessary—to
the west.*[1]

—Piers Paul Read, *Alive*

Nando Parrado watched as the boys wept. When they heard the garbled
news from the barely functioning radio that the search for the downed airplane carrying the Uruguayan rugby team had been terminated, despair
swept through the camp. No one was coming to save them. No one would
help. They were alone.

Just hours before, many had done the unthinkable. On the brink of
starvation, the group decided they had no choice but to indulge in their
first taste of human flesh. But what many thought was a temporary neces-
sity now became crucial to survival. With no hope of rescue, if you want
to live, you eat.

As the other survivors drifted between despair and defiance, Parrado
looked to the mountain. Before the pilot succumbed to his chest wounds,
he had told the survivors that Chile was to the west. But they had a problem. The airplane had crashed into a gentle valley facing east. To the west
stood a nearly impassable mountain.

Parrado's eyes filled with cold resolution. When the radio finished relaying the death sentence, he immediately told his teammates he was leaving to climb the mountain. Uproar ensued as his team begged him to wait. It wasn't ten days earlier that they had left Parrado for dead. He was in no shape to make the deadly climb.

Parrado relented but never took his eyes off the mountain.[2]

The Wild is an unforgiving force. It requires even the best brands to face the raw power of incessant uncertainty and ambiguity. Shrewd leaders anticipate The Wild and prepare their teams to pause in the midst of the storm and find their bearings. But even the wisest leaders may find their triage tactics lacking without the enduring power of focus.

Focus is the antithesis of The Wild. Where The Wild paralyzes, focus empowers. Where The Wild is ambiguity, focus is clarity. The Wild beats you down even to the point of losing your sense of self. Focus is built on uncommon self-awareness. And while The Wild overwhelms with unknowable amounts of information, focus takes advantage of few, but powerful, points of insight.

To find and retain focus requires a strange mix of discipline and faith in the midst of uncontrollable circumstances. Distraction will tempt you at every step, and you will be required to embrace fear. You must accept that focus is achieved more by adhering to a state of mind than arriving at a destination.

Be warned. Focus is hard. Stopping and finding your bearings may not be easy, but it is prescriptive. The path to focus touches on higher-order questions around truth and purpose. Not everyone is willing or able to tackle these questions. And when facing The Wild, your faith in your focus will be tested to the limit.

The great enemy of focus is distraction, a foe Joe Kane wrestled with every day. When we left Kane in Chapter 2, he was clinging to a slippery two-story boulder above the raging Amazon River like a slug on a wall of salt. Every time he tried to get a grip, he would slip across the wet sur-face. He had just made a classic error; in his moment of peril, he looked down and froze. Fifteen feet above the river and a certain death, Kane couldn't move.

Zbigniew Bzdak, one of Kane's companions on the 1985 Amazon Source to Sea Expedition, was just three feet away. Yet Kane wrote that he felt "cut off and alone." Bzdak tried yelling something to Kane, but the clamor of the river made communication impossible. Bzdak inched his way back to Kane, placed his mouth right next to Kane's ear, and screamed "DON'T LOOK DOWN!"[3]

As you navigate The Wild, distraction is your constant enemy. Bzdak's advice seems simple, but in the moment, the raging river can feel impossible to ignore. As we explored in Chapter 2, focusing on fear can actually increase the likelihood of the feared thing happening. The wisdom of "don't look down" can't be overstated. You are where you look. If you're focused on what can go wrong, not only are you making it more likely to happen, you are taking precious attention away from the next outcrop of rock you'll need to climb to safety.

In the mid 1990s, LEGO management "looked down" at the Millennial generation and was terrified. Based on research at the time, LEGO leadership believed the up-and-coming digital natives with a penchant for distraction couldn't handle the attention and skill required to put together traditional LEGO sets. This belief initiated a series of moves that revealed a deep insecurity about the company's core purpose.

Based on the research, LEGO increased the size of its blocks to make them easier to use[4] and pursued a flailing product strategy that resulted in an explosion in complexity, growing from roughly 6,000 total construction set parts to more than 12,000. Then the company rehauled its entire design approach by firing legacy designers who had created product for the past three decades. Instead, LEGO turned to thirty new designers hired straight out of the best design schools in the world.[5] These highly talented graduates, while brilliant, had no experience in toy making and had very little familiarity playing with LEGO products.

LEGO then drifted from its core toy business altogether, splitting its focus among a litany of line extensions, including video games, theme parks, clothing, and more.[6] The distractions culminated in the infamous Galidor toy set, a much-maligned product, based on a children's television show, that looked more like a G.I. Joe knockoff than a traditional LEGO construction set.

By the mid 2000s, the toy maker was on the brink of bankruptcy, clinging to a metaphorical wall above a raging river and focusing on everything but the next slippery lip of rock in front of it. Jørgen Vig Knudstorp, LEGO's CEO at the time, was quoted by Martin Lindstrom as saying, "We are on a burning platform, losing money with negative cash flow, and a real risk of debt default which could lead to a breakup of the company."[7]

LEGO was distracted, firing, diminishing, and running away from everything that made it special in the first place. And when facing The Wild, distraction is death.

Use Fear to Find Focus

Colin Fletcher stood in awe of the desert. His attempt to be the first person to hike the Grand Canyon from end to end had turned into a grueling adventure filled with endless thirst, pain, and fear. In a fleeting moment, every detail of the empty desertscape suddenly clicked into place, revealing an intricate, energized ecosystem. He watched as the desert slid, buzzed, and whirled around him. A lizard leapt in slow motion onto a rock. A butterfly slowed the beating of its wings to reveal their beauty. A hummingbird hovered in, causing the butterfly to alight. It was as if the scales fell from Colin's eyes. He was, as he called it, "knife edge alive."[8]

Jon Krakauer is another prolific adventurer who documented the "knife-edge alive" experience. Krakauer is famous for his harrowing account of the 1996 Everest debacle, *Into Thin Air*, but few are aware of his foolish attempt to solo climb the Devil's Thumb, one of North America's most difficult peaks. Alone and hanging from a sheer ice wall

3,000 feet above the ground, Jon literally faced the abyss. He would later recount his experience:

> Early on a difficult climb, especially a difficult solo climb, you're hyperaware of the abyss pulling at your back. You constantly feel its call, its immense hunger. To resist takes a tremendous conscious effort; you don't dare let your guard down for an instant. The siren song of the void puts you on edge, it makes your movements tentative, clumsy, herky-jerky. But as the climb goes on, you grow accustomed to the exposure, you get used to rubbing shoulders with doom, you come to believe in the reliability of your hands and feet and head. You learn to trust your self-control.
>
> By and by, your attention becomes so intensely focused that you no longer notice the raw knuckles, the cramping thighs, the strain of maintaining nonstop concentration. A trance-like state settles over your efforts, the climb becomes a clear-eyed dream. Hours slide by like minutes. The accrued guilt and clutter of the day-to-day existence . . . is temporarily forgotten, crowded from your thoughts by an overpowering clarity of purpose, and by the seriousness of the task at hand.[9]

Fletcher and Krakauer's "knife-edge alive" experiences represent a well-documented phenomenon in the wilderness, only made possible through unusual levels of fear and isolation. According to the *U.S. Air Force Survival Manual*, fear can paralyze you, or it can be used to find an intense form of focus. "Whether [survivors] will panic from fear, or use it as a stimulant for greater sharpness," the *USAFSM* says, "is more dependent on the survivor's reactions to the situation than on the situation itself."[10]

Strangely, just as companies like LEGO can lose focus because of fear, fear also has the power to bring powerful clarity. As the *USAFSM* points out, it is not the situation itself that determines whether you are driven to paralysis or clarity but your reaction to it.

For the stranded Uruguayan rugby players who learned that rescue would not be coming, fear inspired clarity. A new purpose arose within their ranks. The general disarray that marked much of the early days after the crash settled into disciplined determination. To escape, they must survive. And to survive, they must have order.

The group split up duties, including cutting and cooking meat and cleaning the airplane fuselage. Although Parrado was urged to be patient, the team still knew they must send an expedition to try to find help, and they began identifying the few among them strong enough to make the trip. Somehow, abandonment brought clarity, and clarity created optimism. With no rescue in sight, they either attempted what many thought to be an impossible journey across the mountain or they died a slow death. No in between. No argument. Fear brought focus.[11]

Similarly, as LEGO began hemorrhaging cash in the early 2000s, fear motivated action. Knudstorp was brought in to lead the monumental task of renewing creativity and bringing some semblance of fiscal responsibility to the company. LEGO also brought back famed consultant Martin Lindstrom, a longtime advisor with a deep LEGO history, and began a research-driven journey to rediscover what was truly at the core of the LEGO experience.

As LEGO endured fear, humiliation, and isolation, its story could easily have ended like those of most organizations in its situation, with paralysis followed by death. Instead, the LEGO team used fear to pursue the only thing that could save them: focus.

Return to Focus

Twenty-seven remaining Andes crash survivors heard the news that the rescue was cancelled. Enjoying some semblance of order, the group made their way to the plane for another night in the frigid cold. They finally agreed to a system in which the wounded could find a level of comfort while sleeping and the strong traded spaces near the especially cold entrance. With renewed enthusiasm, they plotted an escape plan, discussing and planning every potential route to civilization.

The night drew on until a loud muffled noise like metal falling to the snow made a boy named Roy suddenly stand up. An instant later, he was chest high in snow.[12] An avalanche filled the fuselage to the brim with cold death. A frantic search began, as most of the group lay under suffocating snow. No one could see. Most could not breathe. One survivor was freed, then another, until many hands dug desperately for the remaining buried. It wasn't enough. Eight more survivors died in a cold, dark instant.

The remaining nineteen lay trapped in the fuselage, waiting for the night to end so they could dig their way out. The cold forced them to punch and kick each other to stimulate circulation. Some wished they had died in the avalanche. Others felt their resolution to escape only deepen.[13]

Following the avalanche, conversations about the escape became an obsession. Several floated theories on how best to manage it, guessing the valley that faced east would eventually turn west or that just on the other side of the towering mountain lay help. The only thing they knew for sure was a piece of information that the pilot shared before he succumbed to his wounds. As Piers Paul Read put it in *Alive*, "over and over again they would repeat the only fact they knew to be true: 'To the west is Chile.' "

When navigating an uncertain situation, cling to what truth you have like a candle in the dark. Truth is the beginning of focus and the enemy of The Wild. The Andes survivors had plenty of theories, but they only had one truth: "to the west is Chile." Unlike the ceaseless ambiguity The Wild throws at you, truth never changes. When you have it, never let it go. When you don't, seek it relentlessly.

LEGO's first error was to believe a lie. Looking at research at the time, management believed the dawn of the digital age, combined with the advent of the ADHD–ridden, pleasure-seeking Millennial generation, meant they must change the company's fundamental value in the eyes of its customers. Based on that lie, management abandoned LEGO's core competency and tried to make LEGO something it wasn't.

To his credit, Knudstorp, in one of his first acts as CEO, sought out the truth behind LEGO's value. He immediately began a new approach to product design that incorporated longtime adult fans, even going as far as hiring the best as on-staff designers. Explaining the purpose behind his new approach to incorporating fans, Knudstorp told the *Harvard Business Review*, "They are an avenue to the truth. And in today's world, a CEO needs every avenue to the truth that he or she can find."[14]

Using the help of advisor Martin Lindstrom, LEGO embarked on an ethnographic study to try to rediscover what made its toys special. The methodology was simple. The team set out to observe children playing in their homes with LEGO products and to ask follow-up questions. An important turning point for LEGO was a minor observation made in an eleven-year-old boy's room in Germany.

During the site visit to the boy's home, one of the researchers noticed a pair of beaten-up sneakers in the room and asked about them. The boy told the researcher that they were his most prized possession, as he was considered one of the best skateboarders in the city, and the beaten-up, rag-tag pair of shoes proved it.

The conversation stunned the team, as it challenged everything they had believed to that point. Millennials weren't lazy digital do-nothings but skill-minded storytellers whose social currency was mastery of a subject matter and a "trophy" that proved it. Writing about the experience, Lindstrom explained, "What executives found out that day was that everything they thought they knew, or had been told, about late twentieth—and early twenty-first-century children and their new digital behaviors—including the need for time compression and instantaneous results—was wrong."[15]

Looking back, the insight that children enjoy a challenge and want to show off their skills seems almost mundane. But when a company is lost, even the simplest truths are hard to see. As LEGO's experience shows, very rarely do companies need to find some new, mysterious truth. They simply need to return to what made them special in the first place. Focus is rarely about changing. Focus is about returning to truth.

That said, while truth is the foundation of everything, truth alone is not enough to find focus. After you discover truth, you must find your brand purpose. Focus is a by-product of brand purpose and cannot exist outside of it. Put another way, purpose is a prerequisite of focus. For many lost brands, survival is the only purpose they know. They are unwilling or unable to look beyond the immediate need to eat for another day.

The healthiest brands exist not just to survive but to thrive. Describing LEGO's journey to rekindle growth, Knudstorp told the *HBR* that to "optimize the firm's value . . . we had to ask, Why does Lego Group exist? Ultimately, we determined the answer: to offer our core products, whose unique design helps children learn systematic, creative problem solving—a crucial twenty-first-century skill."[16]

When LEGO rediscovered the truth, it sought purpose by asking the ultimate question: "Why?" If you answer that question by saying, "To make money," you will have the same basic purpose that every other organization has. Instead, notice that Knudstorp gave a specific, narrow, actionable purpose couched between internal and external truth:

Internal truth: "to offer our core products, whose unique design . . .
Purpose: . . . helps children learn systematic, creative problem solving . . .
External truth: . . . a crucial twenty-first-century skill."

LEGO found its purpose at the intersection of a truth about what it fundamentally does and a relevant customer truth. LEGO's purpose had always been there. It just needed to be identified, celebrated, and matched with a market need.

The fundamental question for brands seeking purpose is "Why?" Why do you exist? Why do you get up in the morning? Why do you do what you do? Asking why is a top-down approach that is effective for many. Another method is to work from the bottom up by asking three sequential questions:

1. "What are we really good at doing?"
2. "What does our customer really need?"
3. "Where do the two intersect?"

The intersection between the truth about your brand and the truth about your customers' needs is where you will find purpose.

Equipped with purpose, LEGO had a focus that was almost obvious. The best way to help children learn creative problem solving was to return to the unique design the company was known for. LEGO found focus not by changing but by returning to what it does best: building awesome toys.

Stay Focused with "No"

The remaining Andes survivors focused all of their energy on preparing a select few to make the perilous hike out. Three of the strongest among them, including Nando Parrado, Roberto Canessa, and Antonio Vizintin, were eventually selected and given special treatment. While the others toiled to prepare the daily food, melt water, tend to the wounded, and clean camp, the expeditionaries were encouraged to eat extra portions, refrain from too much work, and sleep as long as they would like.[17]

The death of another of the wounded survivors brought urgency to an already dire situation. They could wait no longer. It was now or possibly never for many in the group. The morning of the expedition's departure took on a somber tone. Silence surrounded the camp as the chosen hikers ate their breakfast. They would set off at once to try to climb the towering mountain.

The three hikers set off with the goal to reach the summit by night, but as the day turned to dusk, they felt as though they were no nearer the top of the mountain than when they left. During the day's hike, Vizintin nearly fell off a cliff, barely escaping by dropping his backpack at the last second. Canessa had his own near miss when a boulder careened by his head, knocked loose by Parrado's boots.[18]

By now, the hike up the mountain was almost vertical, making finding a campsite nearly impossible. That night the three were forced to huddle together on the face of the mountain, begging for morning.

Just as the light of the sun first peeked over the eastern horizon, Canessa saw it. He couldn't be sure, but far off to the east, he thought he spotted a road. The ambiguous sighting split the group, as Parrado and Vizintin could make out a line in the distance but could not tell whether it was a road.

An argument erupted about the expedition's next move. Canessa viewed the mountain climb as suicidal, citing the previous day's debacles. Parrado couldn't argue with Canessa's fears but wasn't sure the line was a road. Canessa insisted. They must turn back. To the east was a road and salvation. Documenting Canessa and Parrado's heated exchange, Read wrote:

> "And what do we do if we go back?" asked Parrado.
> "Go to the road" [Canessa said].
> "It might be a road," said Parrado, "and it might not; but there's one thing we know for certain. To the west is Chile."

Focus is never safe. It is under constant assault by "distant roads" that promise less risk and an easier path to success. Constant vigilance and confidence found in truth and purpose are the only things standing between you and distraction.

Focus in action is far more about what you don't do than about what you do. For every "yes," focus says a thousand "nos." Knudstorp explained that LEGO's first "no" came with a decision "to compete not by being the biggest but by being the best."[19] After finding focus, the embattled brand immediately began cutting its product suite and exiting expensive distractions like video games, theme parks, and action figures.

LEGO then moved to reinvest in its core construction sets by hiring or promoting new product-centric designers, including several AFOLs (adult fans of LEGO). To make the construction sets relevant again to the challenge-hungry Millennial youth, LEGO reduced the size of blocks to their previous size and even added new challenges to the sets themselves.

A renewed focus on profitable alliances with successful franchises like Star Wars also paid dividends. By 2014, after the release of *The LEGO Movie*, LEGO had grown sales to more than $2 billion, making it the world's largest toy maker.[20]

Mark Stafford, a LEGO designer and one of the AFOLs hired to rethink the company's product suite, expressed the company's return to focus as well as anyone, saying, "It's not just a toy, it's a tool for creation and imagination and getting LEGO bricks into the hands of kids is the only aim of everything we do."[21]

To the West Is Chile

Nando Parrado's shaky hand reached over the crest, clawing dirt and rock to pull himself to the top of the towering mountain. He made it. The sheer mountain walls were behind him. Canessa and Vizintin were below, waiting breathlessly for any word of his success.

Parrado lifted his gaze to see the signs of civilization and salvation that the survivors so desperately needed. But the signs were not there. Before him stretched endless mountaintops. For the first time since crash landing in the frozen wasteland known as the Andes, Parrado's heart sank with despair.[22]

And then he saw it. Much farther to the west, he could just make out the top of a mountain that wasn't covered in ice. Below was a valley that split like a Y. He shook off his despair and made up his mind that this valley would be the destination. Parrado called Canessa up with a shout of victory. But Canessa found it hard to match his companion's enthusiasm. Through another heated exchange, the two reasoned that the journey could take many days, but if they let Vizintin return to camp and shared his rations, the two of them might just have enough supplies to hike to the Y. The three agreed and said their goodbyes.

Parrado and Canessa shot down the western slope of the mountain like butter on a hot pan. The two tumbled down the mountain over shale and loose rock until they came upon a steep and snow-covered section. They then used cushions, brought on the hike for their many uses, including warmth, to act as makeshift sleds, which allowed them to reach speeds as high as sixty miles an hour. Twenty-four hours later, they were near the bottom of the mountain, looking west toward the Y.

Minutes turned to hours, which turned to days. The two remaining members of the expedition grew more desperate by the moment, as each grueling minute in the freezing wilderness sapped their strength and cut into their dwindling supplies. Canessa was emaciated and nearing the end, but Parrado's determination carried them on. Finally, the valley that formed the Y from atop the mountain came into view.

With every step toward the end of the valley, a clamor rose in the background. At first it sounded like a trickle and then a swell and then a chorus. Piers Paul Read captured the moment when Parrado turned the corner at the end of the valley, writing, "The view which met his eyes was of paradise."[23] Parrado lifted his gaze to see the rush of running water pouring over boulders towards the west. The blistering snow was replaced with vegetation and a white-topped river.

Just a few short days later, Parrado's "paradise" would lead to a small courtyard—there, he and Canessa would sit devouring cheese, bread, and scraps of meat. The local ranchers who found them on the edge of town called for rescue, which set out for them and their fellow teammates still stranded in the mountains. It had been ten days since they left camp to hike the mountain and seventy days since the crash.[24]

Focus is hard. It can masquerade as distraction and sit just on the other side of paralyzing fear. But if you are true to it, it will be true to you. Focus can only be found if it rests on truth. Just as the Andes crash survivors looked to the west and LEGO rebuked the lies about its Millennial customer base, you too can find truth. Armed with the facts, however small, turn them into action by finding brand purpose then practicing vigilance. Your thousands of "nos" may just allow your "yes" to lead to paradise.

Survival Tips for Practical Application

Stopping and orienting will only get you so far without the enduring power of focus. Return to focus to navigate the endless distractions of The Wild.

Keep in Mind

- Distraction in the wilderness leads to death.
- Fear can either paralyze or create intense focus.
- Focus is about returning, not changing.

Survival Tips

To navigate The Wild:

- Use fear to foster focus.
- Find the truth in your brand and about your customer.
- Ask "why?" to determine your brand purpose.
- Look for overlap between internal and external truths to help identify your brand purpose.
- Protect your focus by saying "no" to distractions vigilantly.

Notes

1. Piers Paul Read, *Alive: Sixteen Men, Seventy-Two Days, and Insurmountable Odds—the Classic Adventure of Survival in the Andes* (New York: Harper Perennial, 2005), 86–87.
2. Read, *Alive*, 86–87.
3. Joe Kane, *Running the Amazon* (New York: Vintage Books, 1990), 166.
4. Martin Lindstrom, "LEGO Engineered a Remarkable Turnaround of Its Business. How'd That Happen?" *LinkedIn*, March 5, 2016, https://www.linkedin.com/pulse/lego-engineered-remarkable-turnaround-its-business-howd-lindstrom.
5. Richard Feloni, "How Lego Came Back from the Brink of Bankruptcy," *Businessinsider.com*, February 10, 2014, http://www.businessinsider.com/how-lego-made-a-huge-turnaround-2014-2.
6. Lindstrom, "LEGO Engineered a Remarkable Turnaround of Its Business. How'd That Happen?"
7. Lindstrom, "LEGO Engineered a Remarkable Turnaround of Its Business. How'd That Happen?"
8. Colin Fletcher, *The Man Who Walked through Time* (New York: Vintage Books, 1989), 92.
9. Jon Krakauer, *Eiger Dreams: Ventures among Men and Mountains* (Guilford: Lyons Press, 2009), 177–178.
10. *U.S. Air Force Survival Manual*, 52.
11. Read, *Alive*, 119.
12. Read, *Alive*, 121.
13. Read, *Alive*, 130–131.
14. Andrew O'Connell, "Lego CEO Jørgen Vig Knudstorp on Leading through Survival and Growth," *Harvard Business Review*, January 2009, https://hbr.org/2009/01/lego-ceo-jorgen-vig-knudstorp-on-leading-through-survival-and-growth.
15. Lindstrom, "LEGO Engineered a Remarkable Turnaround of Its Business. How'd That Happen?"
16. O'Connell, "Lego CEO Jørgen Vig Knudstorp on Leading through Survival and Growth,"
17. Read, *Alive*, 139.
18. Read, *Alive*, 241.

19. O'Connell, "Lego CEO Jørgen Vig Knudstorp on Leading through Survival and Growth."
20. Lindstrom, "LEGO Engineered a Remarkable Turnaround of Its Business. How'd That Happen?"
21. Mark Safford, comment on Redit, https://www.reddit.com/r/lego/comments/1x6ldp/lego_franchise_infographic/cf8vdl3?st=irnv7gxu&sh=db1c6d53.
22. Read, *Alive*, 245.
23. Read, *Alive*, 285.
24. Read, *Alive*, 304.

CHAPTER 9

Flow

[B]e formless. Shapeless, like water. If you put water into a cup, it becomes the cup. You put water into a bottle and it becomes the bottle. You put it in a teapot, it becomes the teapot. Now, water can flow or it can crash. Be water, my friend.[1]

—*Bruce Lee*

The smell of burning flesh repulsed Autumn Veatch. She let go of her grandfather's seat buckle, repelled by the intense heat. Her hand, face, hair, and eyebrows burned and shriveled, she staggered back in terror. The lonely screams of her dying grandparents echoed through the forest. No one but Veatch could hear the desperate cries.

Surrounded by fog with no access to GPS, Leland and Sharon Bowman and their granddaughter had been flying blind before crashing into the wilderness. As the small prop plane slammed through pine tree after pine tree until finally reaching an abrupt stop in the Montana forest, the Bowmans' cries turned from screams to wails to silence.

Alone and afraid, Veatch began to sob and run. She started down a hill that led to a small cliff and fell flat on her back. It was then she knew she needed to stop and think. Natalie Krebs, writing for *Outdoor Life*, documented what ran through the young girl's mind, saying she "recalled the survival shows she had watched with her dad in grade school—shows like *Man vs. Wild* and *Dual Survival*. The two main principles she remembered were to travel downhill and follow water."[2]

Moments later, Veatch quieted herself and listened. She thought she could hear the rumblings of civilization. Instead, she would find a river.

Navigating uncertainty is the chief challenge facing brands in today's economy. We no longer operate in a business environment in which size, strength, scale, intellectual property, or longevity provide a sustainable competitive advantage. The increasing pace of disruption resulting from the ubiquity of information and the education and mobility of the workforce has changed everything. So prepare to disrupt. Or be disrupted.

Chris Taylor, a business executive and former U.S. Navy pilot, discussed the fundamental shift from the principles that fueled the Industrial Age to the new principles that drive the Age of Disruption in an article on *VentureBeat*, writing, "Disruption isn't just a phase we're going through. Disruption replaces the industrial concepts of the 1800s and 1900s with faster cycles of change coming with lower levels of investment and risk."[3]

Disruption isn't a passing trend. Disruption is the new normal. Uncertainty and continuous change are here to stay. The only way to thrive in the new economy is to prepare for the unexpected. But how can you prepare for something unpredictable? Who has the resources and capacity to prepare for every eventuality? Or, as John Wiseman put it in *The SAS Survival Handbook*, "How can you prepare for what you do not expect?" and "[W]hat chance have you of equipping yourself for the totally unknown disaster?"[4]

In truth, you can't. Nobody has the time, money, or prescience to prepare for every potentiality. And those who try are effectively paralyzed. If there is anything we have learned from history it is that Great Walls crumble, castles are starved, and Maginot Lines are circumvented. Static strength is weakness waiting to be exposed. Just as Autumn Veatch remembered while lost in the Montana forest, water is life in the wilderness. To effectively navigate uncertainty, it's of no help to be a rock. You must be a river.

Resilience, not strength, is the new competitive advantage. You cannot prepare for every detail and eventuality. To succeed, you must augment your skill set with a set of principles that prepare you to thrive in any environment, regardless of the details on the ground. Just like the expert survivalist who can be dropped into a desert, a forest, or a frozen tundra and always find a way to survive, you must have a resilient core complemented by a flexible mode of operation that transcends challenges.

Wiseman asserts that this resilient core allows you to deal with constantly changing environments, writing that you must "know about a whole range of skills which can be applied and adapted to all kinds of situations and to develop a way of thinking that enables you to draw upon them to find the solutions to particular problems. This is the preparation you can make for the unexpected."[5]

The solution to uncertainty lies not in the details but in the ability to rise above the details and adapt to any situation. In the wilderness, water is the one enduring substance that can be detoured but never defeated. Water is a master of adaptation. It is the only natural matter that can operate as a liquid, a solid, and a gas.[6] It can absorb incredible amounts of heat, which is one of the reasons life can flourish on earth.[7] And it is practically the only substance in existence that will contract when cooled until a certain point at which it, incredibly, starts to expand.[8]

Water has such powers of adaptation because it operates with both structure and freedom. You can scorch water, freeze it, or try to slow it down, but it will always find a way to achieve its singular goal: get to the ocean. No matter how water transforms to overcome an obstacle, it never loses its "waterness." Whether it separates, shrinks, expands, or flows, it is always water, and it will always advance toward its goal. It is at once itself and anything it needs to be. In a word, it is fluid, as both a noun and an adjective.

To navigate The Wild, you must be too.

Liquid Branding

Autumn Veatch's world turned upside down when her grandparents' plane lost a GPS signal in the fog and crashed into the Montana wilderness.

Lying on her back after falling over a small cliff, she gathered her wits and forced herself to be still, observe her surroundings, and orient herself by following the sound of what she initially thought was civilization.

She found the river and spent hours following it, crossing over when necessary. As the hour grew late, she knew she couldn't continue in the dark and found a place to rest for the night. But as the sun dipped below the horizon, she realized that crossing the river might have been a bad decision. Her clothes were soaking wet, and the cold made sleep impossible. She took most of her clothing off, laid it out to dry, and tried to warm herself in her cardigan. Fear of hypothermia consumed her thinking the entire night.

When the sun finally turned the black night to gray morning, Veatch set out to continue down the river. But after only a few minutes, her heart sank. She was lost, alone, and completely out of her element. She found the nearest tree and lay down beneath its drooping branches to die.[9]

To be a fluid brand, you must shift your perspective on disruption, thinking of it not as an enemy but as an opportunity. Disruption is not the problem; your reaction to it is. If you try to be rock, you're likely to crack, break, and perhaps be reduced to dust. If you are water, however, you'll see endless opportunities to flow past problems. Most brands are rocks.

The key to learning how a brand can operate like water begins with an obscure Air Force pilot and military strategist named John Boyd. Boyd was an ace fighter pilot who earned the nickname "40-Second Boyd" during the Korean War for offering every new pilot a challenge. Boyd claimed that he could start a dogfight with his aircraft in front of any pilot and be on his tail within forty seconds. If he lost, he would pay $40. He never had to pay.[10]

Boyd's theorems radically altered every air force in the world.[11] They were critical to the development of the F-16 and other aircraft and culminated in his architecture of the Desert Storm "Left Hook" strategy, making Boyd what some consider one of the greatest military minds in history.

During his time in the Korean War, Boyd observed a surprising phenomenon. Although he and his fellow pilots flew comparably less maneuverable aircraft, they consistently won dogfights with their enemy, who flew quick and nimble Russian-made MIG-15s. Boyd believed this was due to the fact that the American F-86 had a better field of vision.[12]

This observation would lead to the development of the OODA Loop. OODA stands for observe, orient, decide, and act. Boyd held that, in every threatening or unfamiliar situation, a person or group continually cycles through all four stages of the loop as they make a decision. In the Korean War dogfights, Boyd postulated that the American pilots who flew inferior aircraft won more often because they were disrupting their opponents' OODA Loop by having advantages in observation and orientation.[13] In other words, even though the MIG-15s were superior aircraft in almost every way, the Americans were better equipped to adapt. The Koreans were trapped inside their superior technology like a rock in a river, so the Americans flowed right past.

By understanding and optimizing each step in the OODA Loop, brands can learn to quickly adapt to disruption or create their own and, by doing so, paralyze competitors who may enjoy traditional advantages.

Observe is the first step in the OODA Loop. It consists of gathering information about your surroundings and the danger they pose. The focus is to gather as much accurate information as possible from both internal and external sources to create an assessment of the situation at hand.

Orient is the second and potentially most important step of the OODA Loop. In this step, you are interpreting the observed information that will provide the basis for judgments to come. How you orient affects what you decide and how you act, which in turn affects future observation.

Decide is the step in which you make a hypothesis about what course of action to take based on your observation and interpretation of the facts. Once you form a hypothesis, it is time to act.

Act is the final step, in which you test your hypothesis and prepare to cycle back through the OODA Loop. Based on the data gathered from your test, you once again observe and interpret the facts and again complete the cycle. In a dogfight, OODA Loop cycles are mere seconds long. In the wilderness, they may take minutes or hours. If you're lucky, your brand may have the luxury of days or even weeks.

The purpose of OODA is to understand the basic steps of how your brand and your competition make decisions. If a brand can optimize each step in its loop, it can move faster and make better decisions. Writing on the topic, Chris Taylor reflects the benefits of taking an OODA Loop approach in the Age of Disruption, saying, "The nimble business—behaving as an innovation lab, operating in tight iterations, and striving to be faster than the adversary—replaces the traditional factory."[14]

Uber's disruption of the taxi industry wasn't magic. The upstart transportation company simply got inside the entrenched system's OODA Loop. With a status quo that enabled taxi operators to become noted for bad service and high costs, Uber saw an opportunity to leverage consumers' deep-seated distaste for every aspect of the experience, including hailing a cab.

Consumers had two options to access a cab: walk to a curb or call a phone number. Uber came along and gave consumers a third option: download an app and arrange a ride via smartphone. Quick, affordable ground transportation suddenly became easily accessible from anywhere. And by opening up its driving operations to anyone with a background check and a car, Uber was also able to operate at a fraction of competitors' overhead. Uber's emphasis on agility has allowed it to overcome the entrenched strength of its more powerful competition and force them to restart their OODA Loop. Uber is water. The taxi industry is rock. In the wilderness, water beats rock.

Understanding the salience of each step in the OODA Loop is crucial, as each can change in importance over time. In the Industrial Age, observation offered significant competitive advantage. Data was limited, and those who held it could leverage it to their advantage. In today's digital world, observation is declining as a comparative advantage because of the abundance of information available to companies large and small. Access to information is cheap.

By contrast, orientation is growing as a strategic advantage. Keith H. Hammonds discusses the phenomenon in a piece for *Fast Company*, postulating that

> the wide, instantaneous availability of data creates an environment of complete transparency. In such a world, it would be impossible to gain advantage from observation, since all competitors would see the same thing. Orientation, then, would grow even more important: The data is worthless, after all, without our interpretation.[15]

In the OODA Loop, action may be losing its advantage as well, as automation makes certain functions move at incredible speed, and artificial intelligence and robotics replicate human skill with increasing accuracy. This phenomenon explains the devaluation of "doers" in many domains and the increased value of systems design. But the robots still need to be told what to do, putting a premium on decision. Orientation and decision may be the two stages in the OODA Loop that provide the Age of Disruption's competitive advantage.

In the end, the goal of understanding the OODA Loop is, like Boyd's heroic fighter pilots, to optimize your loop in order to get inside that of your opponent. The more you can use the OODA Loop to adapt like water, the more effective you will be at transforming your opponents into rock. By forcing them to observe and reorient themselves to a situation of your making, you buy yourself precious time to gain further advantage. Terry Deitz, a former U.S. Navy F-14 pilot and business consultant, explained OODA disruption to *VentureBeat*, saying, "In warfare and in business, the speed at which the OODA Loop is executed becomes the largest factor in disrupting the enemy in the battle space, and the competition in the business space." Speed, then, outperforms strength.

Liquid Brands Have Structured Freedom

Agility, although vital, is not enough for today's multilayered brands to navigate uncertainty. It is easy to interpret agility in branding as simply empowering teams to move faster by removing rules and roadblocks, but that path, in isolation, can lead to organizational chaos. Conversely, although water can adapt to any situation, it always acts with singular purpose within a certain set of rules. It is freedom within structure that unleashes the true power of liquid branding.

After developing the OODA Loop, John Boyd would go on to outline the principles necessary to operate with both structure and freedom. His principles hold true for the complex ecosystems that are today's brands.

Boyd was considered a thorn in the side of many in leadership during his career in the U.S. military. Although he contributed more to the art of war and advanced strategy than most in the last hundred years, he never earned the rank of general. He was brilliant, and he knew it. That made him arrogant and impatient with the Byzantine bureaucracy that is the modern military.

He also rarely wrote down his theories, choosing instead to communicate them through lengthy in-person oral presentations that could go on for hours. Much of Boyd's thinking has been preserved only because his disciples collected and documented a large number of his handwritten notes, sketches, and presentations.[16]

One of John Boyd's most important theses is called Patterns in Conflict. The last known version to exist is dated 1986. It has since been augmented and updated by Boyd's closest colleagues to protect and enshrine his thinking.[17] The document provides an overview of the general stratagems of war, noting key approaches that have evolved through time, including attrition conflict and maneuver conflict.

Attrition conflict culminated in the brutal trench warfare of WWI. It was fundamentally based in brute strength: Line 'em up and knock 'em down. Inflicting maximum damage to the foe in the quickest manner was its chief aim. In this approach to warfare, size, scale, and strength and the ability to use them efficiently against your opponent's weakness was the priority.

Maneuver conflict is best exemplified by the infamous German blitzkrieg during WWII and the menacing warfare waged by Genghis Khan's Mongol empire. It is grounded in concepts of surprise, agility, and speed.

The last one hundred years of business were, in many ways, based on concepts found in attrition conflict. Growth through acquisition and line extension, the pursuit of scale, size as the chief measure of success, and the protection of intellectual property are all based on winning through strength. The cola wars, which saw Coca-Cola and Pepsi go head to head and call each other out, is a perfect example. They lined up their armies and fought in the trenches.

Contrast the stratagems of yesterday with those required to operate in today's economy, and you'll quickly recognize that those approaches represent an anachronism. Size and longevity may even be a sign that you're behind the curve. The old model of centralized command and control doesn't work anymore. The days of trench warfare in marketing are over. Yesterday's business strategy was based on power. Today's is based on adaptability through structured freedom. When uncertainty rules, liquidity reigns.

To achieve structured freedom, the purposes of leadership must be protected while simultaneously empowering frontline teams to adapt to changing circumstances. The only way to understand how to achieve this seemingly contradictory balance of structure and freedom is to appreciate the different OODA Loop speeds found in organizations.

Much like the outer rim of a whirlpool, management's OODA Loops work at a slower pace, as they tackle larger strategic problems with many different information inputs. Frontline teams operate like the quickly spinning center of a whirlpool, working in faster OODA Loops as they deal with the realities on the ground day by day, minute by minute. The key is to maintain cohesion between management and frontline teams so that the goals and parameters set forth by management are respected while employees have the freedom to adapt to changing circumstances.

Boyd outlines this powerful balance in his description of maneuver conflict. The Germans were able to demolish massive armies with inferior numbers at lightning speeds in WWII, and Genghis Khan is famous for creating the impression of enormous firepower with lesser numbers.[18] Boyd says that the speed, agility, and devastating effectiveness of these armies were made possible not just through superior tactics but through the concept of mission, known in modern business terms as internal alignment.

Boyd describes this alignment as "A common outlook . . . [that] . . . represents a unifying theme that can be used to simultaneously encourage subordinate initiative yet realize superior intent."[19] Boyd goes on to explain that

> The German concept of mission can be thought of as a contract, hence an agreement, between superior and subordinate. The subordinate agrees to make his actions serve his superior's intent in terms of what is to be accomplished, while the superior agrees to give his subordinate wide freedom to exercise his imagination and initiative in terms of how intent is to be realized.[20]

In marketing speak, Boyd's "mission" is internal alignment between and among management and employees. Without alignment, second-guessing and unfocused activity create chaos and paralyze organizations. But with it, trust can form between leadership and frontline teams, creating the perfect recipe for adaptation and innovation.

Jørgen Vig Knudstorp, LEGO's CEO and one of the architects of the company's turnaround, discussed the importance of freedom within structure with the *Harvard Business Review*, saying, "Implementing a strategy of niche differentiation and excellence required a looser structure and a relaxation of the top-down management style." Knudstorp went on to say that creativity was vital for growth because "the company's management became quite risk averse while focusing on survival. Now it needs to become opportunity driven, which requires taking greater calculated risks."[21]

To accomplish internal alignment, Boyd suggests three prerequisites, including decentralization, responsibility, and implicit communication. All militaries using maneuver conflict principles exhibit strong leadership executed through decentralized command and control. Implemented correctly, this does not encourage chaos but empowers frontline teams to operate within faster OODA Loops and disrupt the enemy. Built on the trust created through alignment, leadership establishes purpose, goals, focus, and incentives and then gets out of the way to allow their teams to accomplish these goals in the most efficient way possible.

However, the freedom made possible through decentralization comes with a price. It requires employees to carry increased responsibility, take calculated risks, and operate with unusual levels of initiative. And it compels leadership to trust them to do so. This situation is impossible outside of a strong culture that is clearly defined, internally policed, and backed up by efficient hiring practices.

One of the advantages of decentralization and employee responsibility is their emphasis on implicit over explicit communication. If you are trying to create a culture that doesn't exist, you often communicate aspirations over reality. In organizations with low levels of trust, internal communications require enormous effort to both clearly convey expectations and continuously refocus misaligned employees. In organizations with strong alignment and trust, management and employees alike understand how they are expected to act in every situation, requiring less explicit communication and allowing the organization to reduce internal friction and focus on the task at hand.

Boyd's OODA Loop and concept of mission empower adaptation and alignment, the chemical formula for liquid branding. With the resulting structured freedom in place, your brand is able to give management the time needed to run through its slower OODA Loop cycle while empowering frontline teams to rapidly adapt to changing circumstances through faster OODA Loop cycles. The intel gathered through faster frontline OODA Loops can in turn fuel better management decisions, enabling your brand to continuously operate inside your competitor's OODA Loops and keep them off balance—like water over rock.

The River of Life

Autumn Veatch wanted to die. Lying beneath a tree, she was lost, alone, and ready to give up. But after forty-five minutes languishing on the ground, she got mad. Her will to live kicked in. She felt she had so much more to do in life. She couldn't die now.

To find her way out of the wilderness, Veatch returned to the river. As she followed the water, her emotions rose and sank between hope and despair. She sang. She prayed. She talked. She thought of her loved ones back home. As another long day of hiking turned to night, she lay down alongside the river to sleep. But again, sleep never came. This time it was sand fleas that tortured her exhausted, malnourished body.

The next morning, she was in terrible shape. Her body ached from the crash and her lingering untreated burns. But the internal mantra she kept repeating gave her hope: "travel downhill and follow water."[22] Finally, on the third day, she lifted her gaze to see a wooden bridge above the river. It would lead her to a trailhead parking lot. A few minutes later, a car pulled in.

The 9–1–1 operator recorded her call. "Autumn Veatch . . . V-E-A-T-C-H," she told the dispatcher. "We crashed, and I was the only one that made it out."[23]

As you transform your approach from solid rock to supple liquid, remember that there is a reason most brands can't do it. It requires healthy internal dynamics and an unusual sense of purpose and focus in the marketplace. Liquid branding is not solely about speed but agility. Static strength is not enough. You must continually adapt.

Built on the adaptability and internal alignment that create structured freedom, you can maintain cohesion between management and employee OODA Loops and empower your team to iterate quickly and adjust to ever-changing circumstances. Because, as Boyd put it, "each minute ahead of the enemy is an advantage."[24]

The world is filled with rocks. Be water, my friend.

Survival Tips for Practical Application

In today's Age of Disruption, rely on principles of adaptation and alignment to continually read and react to permanent uncertainty.

Keep in Mind

- The principles that fueled the Industrial Revolution are becoming obsolete.
- Size, scale, and longevity are signs you may be behind the curve.
- Today's successful brands emphasize speed, agility, innovation, and adaptability.
- Resilience, not strength, is the new competitive advantage.

Survival Tips

To navigate The Wild:

- Develop a concept of "mission" to ensure internal alignment and reduce friction.
- Understand your organization's OODA Loops and empower employees to execute their own at faster and faster rates.
- Enable internal alignment through decentralization, employee responsibility, and implicit communication.

Notes

1. "Bruce Lee Quotes," *Goodreads.com*, accessed July 30, 2016, https://www. goodreads.com/author/quotes/32579.Bruce_Lee.
2. Natalie Krebs, "The Crash: The Sole Survivor of a Remote Plane Wreck Rescues Herself," *Outdoor Life*, April 2016, 44.

3. Chris Taylor, "Get Your Organization to Think and Act Like a Fighter Pilot," Venture Beat (blog), February 6, 2013, http://venturebeat.com/2013/02/06/helping-your-organization-move-like-a-fighter-pilot/#Ay73wjQE8mL xmO1F.99.

4. John 'Lofty' Wiseman, *SAS Survival Handbook: The Ultimate Guide to Surviving Anywhere*, 3rd ed. (New York: William Morrow, 2014), 27.

5. Williams, *SAS Survival Handbook*, 27.

6. Philipp Harper, "Things You Didn't Know about Water: For Starters, It's the Same as It Was 3 Billion Years Ago," *NBCNews.com*, accessed July 8, 2016, http://www.nbcnews.com/id/6124627/ns/technology_and_science-science/t/things-you-didnt-know-about-water/.

7. Howard Perlman, "Specific Heat Capacity of Water," *USGS*, May 2, 2016, http://water.usgs.gov/edu/heat-capacity.html.

8. Miranda Marquit, "Why Does Water Expand When It Cool? A New Explanation," *Phys.org*, July 17, 2009, http://phys.org/news/2009–07-cools-explanation.html.

9. Krebs, "The Crash: The Sole Survivor of a Remote Plane Wreck Rescues Herself," 44.

10. Keith H. Hammonds, "The Strategy of the Fighter Pilot," *Fast Company*, May 31, 2002, http://www.fastcompany.com/44983/strategy-fighter-pilot.

11. Brett McKay and Kaye McKay, "The Tao of Boyd: How to Master the OODA Loop," *The Art of Manliness*, September 15, 2014, http://www.artofmanliness.com/2014/09/15/ooda-loop/.

12. David K. Williams, "What a Fighter Pilot Knows about Business: The OODA Loop," *Forbes*, February 19, 2013, http://www.forbes.com/sites/davidkwilliams/2013/02/19/what-a-fighter-pilot-knows-about-business-the-ooda-loop/#5c2bb6b26650.

13. Williams, "What a Fighter Pilot Knows about Business: The OODA Loop."

14. Taylor, "Get Your Organization to Think and Act Like a Fighter Pilot."

15. Hammonds, "The Strategy of the Fighter Pilot."

16. Hammonds, "The Strategy of the Fighter Pilot."

17. John Boyd Compendium, *A Discourse on Winning and Losing: Patterns of Conflict*, PDF, Defense and the National Interest, December 6, 2007, http://www.dnipogo.org/boyd/pdf/poc.pdf.

18. Compendium, *A Discourse on Winning and Losing*, 25–28.

19. Compendium, *A Discourse on Winning and Losing*, 74.

20. Compendium, *A Discourse on Winning and Losing*, 76.

21. Andrew O'Connell, "Lego CEO Jørgen Vig Knudstorp on Leading through Survival and Growth."

22. Krebs, "The Crash: The Sole Survivor of a Remote Plane Wreck Rescues Herself," 44.

23. Krebs, "The Crash: The Sole Survivor of a Remote Plane Wreck Rescues Herself," 45.

24. Compendium, *A Discourse on Winning and Losing*, 79.

CHAPTER 10

Adapt

Companies and people look at the pace of change as a challenge, an obstacle, a hurdle. . . . We like to look at it as opportunity: Get on the offense.[1]

—*Mark Parker, Nike CEO*

The enormous sea creature slammed into the side of the boat like a wrecking ball. Steve Callahan woke to a torrent of water plunging in from the ocean. He stumbled through the darkness and found the inflatable life raft but realized that all of his supplies were still in the quickly sinking sailboat. He dove beneath the waves to get his meager rations of food and water. It took several trips to gather everything, exhausting his frantic muscles. Sitting alone in a six-foot rubber life raft, he spent the rest of the night bailing water with a small tin can, praying for morning.[2]

Callahan had looked forward to crossing the Atlantic his whole life. By the age of twenty-nine, he finally built his own sailboat and successfully made the formidable voyage. He was only a week into his return journey when a large sea creature smashed his boat and sent it to the bottom of the ocean. Callahan was now 800 miles west of the Canary Islands, drifting away from civilization with little more than a couple of flares and a few days' food and water.

It was fourteen seemingly endless, sunbaked days before he even saw another boat. He immediately shot a flare, but the would-be rescuer just sailed away. Two weeks turned into thirty days, which stretched into fifty. Up until this point, no human in recorded history had survived more than thirty days adrift at sea. By now Callahan was fending off madness. He kept a daily log during the ordeal and later wrote that he was "stretched so tight between my body, mind, and spirit that I might snap at any moment." He was convinced that "he might go mad at any time."[3]

On day forty, Callahan's life raft developed a tear. Barely clinging to life, he spent the next ten days bailing water endlessly from the sagging raft. By day fifty, he could go on no longer. His entire being was exhausted beyond limit. He was ready to give up.

Most brands view uncertainty the same way Callahan looked at his perpetually sinking raft, as a problem to be fixed rather than a given to be exploited. We spend most of our time trying to bail out as much uncertainty as possible from our sinking brand, hoping that at some point the ocean will run out of water. In the end, we exhaust ourselves in a futile pursuit of security that doesn't exist.

The truth is that uncertainty is as certain in marketing as it is in life. And in business today, it is just growing and accelerating. Today's most successful brands don't try to avoid or "fix" uncertainty; they embrace it.

Mark Parker, Nike's confident but soft-spoken leader, who was named "The World's Most Creative CEO" by *Fast Company*, sat down with the publication to explain how Nike deals with uncertainty and change. In the interview he emphasized a new mindset, saying,

Things are accelerating. . . . How do you adapt to your environment and really focus on your potential? To really go after that, you have to embrace the reality that it is not going to slow down. And you have to look at that as half full, not half empty.[4]

Embracing uncertainty doesn't mean that you passively accept it. To truly succeed, you must look at uncertainty as a chance to gain an advantage. Parker goes on to say, "We try to help accelerate the change ourselves. . . . If you get that it's an opportunity, you'll want to."

In a hyperconnected world with instantaneous communication, uncertainty reigns. But it doesn't have to be your adversary. The anxiety you feel because of the ceaseless unknowns is shared by everyone, which means whoever can better navigate that common uncertainty gains the advantage. With a firm grasp of the OODA Loop and systems in place that take advantage of constant change, you can adapt when others break.

Exploring the roots of John Boyd's OODA Loop, Grant Hammond, author of *The Mind of War: John Boyd and American Security*, takes the concept of embracing uncertainty even further, writing, "Ambiguity is central to Boyd's vision . . . not something to be feared but something that is a given. . . . We never have complete and perfect information. The best way to succeed is to revel in ambiguity."[5]

Before you can revel in ambiguity, however, you need to understand its unique characteristics. Brett McKay, founder of the Art of Manliness, researched the origins of John Boyd's concepts and identified three principles of uncertainty that provide a basis for how to navigate it. They include Gödel's Incompleteness Theorems, Heisenberg's Uncertainty Principle, and the Second Law of Thermodynamics.[6]

Fundamentally, uncertainty is rooted in a lack of information. To be uncertain is to not know. Ambiguity is related, but different. Ambiguity is rooted in unclear information. You may have information, but it is difficult to interpret. When you look at the world around you, information is never completely clear, knowable, or static. The sooner you fully accept this truth, the sooner you can understand the value of putting systems in place that don't institutionalize static knowledge but allow your processes to continually change as your understanding of information changes.

Gödel's Incompleteness Theorems[7] essentially prove that any understanding of reality is always incomplete and requires ongoing refinement as new information arises. In short, you may know a lot, but you can't completely know.

Heisenberg's Uncertainty Principle goes even further to say that nothing in the universe can be perfectly measured. As Alok Jha, a scientific correspondent for *The Guardian*, put it in an article on the topic, "the uncertainty principle enshrines a level of fuzziness into quantum theory."[8] He goes on to explain that Heisenberg's principle "says that we cannot measure the position (x) and the momentum (p) of a particle with absolute precision." Said another way, you can measure a lot, but you can't perfectly measure.

John Boyd's final inspiration is drawn from the Second Law of Thermodynamics. Among other things, the law states that, in isolation, systems experience entropy, the tendency of all things toward disarray. Brett McKay explains that Boyd observed individuals and groups suffering from the Second Law of Thermodynamics when they operated like a closed system and did not pursue fresh perspectives. McKay goes on to say that "just as a closed system in nature will have increasing entropy, or disorder, so too will a person or organization experience mental entropy or disorder if they're cut off from the outside world and new information."

Combined, Gödel's Incompleteness Theorems, Heisenberg's Uncertainty Principle, and the Second Law of Thermodynamics provide two guiding truths: first, uncertainty and ambiguity are an inherent part of reality, and second, closed systems die. To adapt, you must create a system that enables flexibility and constantly adjusts to new information. Rigid brands are dead brands. Isolated brands are dead brands.

The problem is that most brands are not structured to adapt. Built on principles of the Industrial Revolution, brands tend to emphasize efficiency over adaptability. Business historically pursued the concept of "fixing" uncertainty by bailing out the raft. If today's businesses operate under the same principles, not only will they exhaust themselves, they will eventually sink.

Dave Grey, author of *The Connected Company*, explains that most companies are "tightly coupled," meaning adaptability isn't just hard to accomplish, it may require a fundamental transformation of the underlying structure of the business. He explains:

Most businesses today are not designed with agility in mind . . . [they] are tightly coupled, like trains on a track, in order to maximize control and efficiency. But what the business environment requires today is not efficiency but flexibility. So we have these tightly coupled systems and the rails are not pointing in the right direction. And changing the rails, although we feel it is necessary, is complex and expensive to do. So we sit in these business meetings, setting goals and making our strategic plans, arguing about which way the rails should be pointing, when what we really need is to get off the train altogether and embrace a completely different system and approach.[9]

To make matters worse, many brands today operate like closed systems. It is only natural, as a company grows, finds some level of success, and institutionalizes a culture, that the operation turns insular. Humans are comfortable inside boxes of their own making. The problem is that the Second Law of Thermodynamics, and human experience, shows us that insularity breeds decay.

As the company grows in size, insularity can be even harder to combat. Nike's CEO discussed the challenge of pursuing adaptability in a large organization, saying, "At a big company, often size turns into constipation, it fogs the lens about what's really happening. Sometimes with size and success comes the notion that since we've done things to be successful, we have the formula and can institutionalize it. That can be death."[10]

Thus, brands face two core challenges in the Age of Disruption: overcoming underlying structures that emphasize efficiency over flexibility and avoiding closed systems that foster insularity. Examples of adaptive systems built to overcome these challenges abound. Michael Hendrix, partner at industrial design firm Ideo, thinks musicians hold the key to the new creative economy.[11] In a piece written for *Fast Company*, the modern Mad Man compared his company's adaptive process, called Design Thinking, to an approach one might call "Jazz Thinking," used in many music schools.

Jazz, unlike traditional music genres, emphasizes improvisation and innovation over reading from sheet music. Any good musician will tell you, however, that jazz is one of the hardest forms of music to play well.

It is built on a deep understanding of the fundamental principles of music and requires a team approach that accentuates implicit communication during performances and on-the-fly adaptation to the mood of the crowd and the ideas of bandmates. Jazz doesn't just embrace ambiguity, it doesn't exist without it. Jazz revels in ambiguity.

Today's market leaders must fundamentally change the way they approach business and marketing, deemphasizing top-down command-and-control structures in exchange for nimble teams of highly trained specialists empowered to innovate within a certain set of guidelines. Teams that are still reading from sheet music are stuck in an outmoded model. The future belongs to jazz.

So what does true adaptation amid uncertainty look like? John Boyd used a famous example to explain adaptation and innovation, which Brett McKay outlined while researching Boyd's concepts. Boyd titled his analogy *Strategic Game of ? and ?*,[12] complete with the question marks. During a presentation, Boyd would ask those in the room to imagine being in four completely different environments: on a ski slope with other skiers, in Florida on a motor boat, outside riding a bicycle on a beautiful day, and in a department store with your child looking at toy tractors.[13] Separately, each environment comes with expected connections, like hand warmers on the ski slope or sunscreen in Florida. If you mix elements from different environments together, you create confusion.

Boyd would then ask listeners to choose a single element of each environment and try to make something new. They might take skis from the ski slope, the motor from the boat in Florida, the handlebar from the bike, and the rubber treads from the toy tractor. What do you get? If you are operating as a nimble team empowered to innovate, the seemingly disparate parts come together to create a snowmobile.

Boyd's snowmobile example is a salient illustration of how to operate in today's uncertainty. What historically have been distinct domains of skill and knowledge are now colliding thanks to technology, creating entirely new domains of skill and knowledge. If you operate like an orchestra that is built on central command, order, and efficiency, this chaos scares you. But if you can improvise like a jazz band, ambiguity is simply new information that can improve your jam session.

To survive for fifty days on the endless ocean, Steve Callahan had to master the art of Jazz Thinking. With almost no supply of food and water, Callahan instituted strict rationing, saving his fresh water for the first sign of land. Instead, he drank whatever brackish water he could make. He would fold his shirt three times then strain ocean water into a tin over and over until it turned into a cloudy substance. The resulting "water" was revolting, but it kept him alive.[14]

Before long, the brackish water just made Callahan thirstier. With every drink, his malnourished body demanded more. Nothing could pacify his endless thirst. He developed saltwater sores and became obsessed with the fresh water that he was saving for the first sight of land. Callahan knew he had to find a way to get fresh water. He got to work making a solar still out of whatever scraps of plastic he could find. He formed the materials into a flat, round container and curled up the edges like a "deep-dish pizza."[15] Seawater would then evaporate into mist and collect in the dome, allowing fresh water drops created by condensation of the ocean water to slide down the edges, where he gingerly collected them.

Callahan was also tormented by constant hunger, so he began work improvising a makeshift spear gun out of a butter knife and plastic and wood that floated by. He spent endless hours staring at the ocean beside the boat waiting for the perfect moment to strike. A dorado fish would swim by. Sometimes a small sooty bird would land on the edge of the life raft looking for rest. Miss after miss. Then a hit. He would eat that night.[16]

Much like Steve Callahan, marketers today must be able to make improvised spear guns out of plastic trash and butter knives. That may sound like a tall order, but adaptation actually relies more on a shift in thinking than some sort of innate knowledge or skill. If uncertainty and ambiguity are the problem, then attentiveness and creativity are the solution. To overcome a closed system and enable innovation and adaptability, you need to develop an approach that continually inputs new knowledge, interprets it, and makes it usable.

This system begins with a mode of operation called "Condition Yellow."[17] The late Jeff Cooper, a marine-trained expert in pistol technique, created the well-known color system for situational awareness. Brett McKay describes Cooper's Condition Yellow as being both "relaxed and alert."[18] Although you are relaxed, you are in a state of engaged awareness with your surrounding environment. Law enforcement might use the example of visiting a local coffee shop. You may be relaxing with a friend, but you sit with your back to the wall, are aware of every exit, and monitor patrons for any abnormal behavior.

Condition Yellow is essentially a form of continuous observation in the OODA Loop. For marketers, the challenge is rarely about having access to information, because information is cheap. The challenge is being continually attentive to the right information. Part of the challenge of The Wild is the enormous amount of information it throws at you. Brands today can't possibly hope to gather and interpret all of it. Instead, you must focus on gathering the right people, who interpret the right information for you.

To get to the right information and thrive in the wilderness, you need deep knowledge, curated knowledge, and connected knowledge. You must nurture a network of internal or external experts who curate the knowledge for you. Then you need to make sure the knowledge is accessible when you face a challenge that demands a particular skill set (if you want to make a snowmobile, you have to know a little bit about skiing, boating, biking, and tractors). Today's brands must become curators of curators. Connectors of connections. Networks of networks. A modern brand values connection over internal capability.

Adaptation Requires Native Knowledge

The first step in developing a network is to find deep knowledge. To do so, you go native.

Bertram Thomas, one of the greatest explorers of the Arabian Desert, was in awe of his Bedouin companion's deep knowledge of the wilderness. As the expedition suffered from the heavy desert heat, cracked lips, burned skin, and incessant water obsessions, they took inventory of their most vital possessions: their camels. Thomas documented the back and forth with his Bedouin companion, writing:

> The grouped tracks of four camels walking in line arrested my companion's attention, and he turned to me and asked me in play which camel I saw in the sands to be best. I pointed—pardonably, I persuaded myself—to the wrong one. "There," he said, "do you see that cuffing up of the toes? It is a good sign: but not that skidding," pointing to mine, "between the footmarks." "That," he said of the third, "is an animal that has recently been in the steppe. Do you see the rugged impressions of her feet? Camels that have long been in the sands leave smooth impressions, and that" (pointing to the fourth) "is her baby. Your camel is big with young—see the deep impressions of her small hind feet." And thus and thus. It was not the least important part of Hamad's lore—a lore shared by nearly every dweller of the sands in varying degree—to read the condition of the strange camel, as yet unseen, from her marks, and hence to know whether to flee or to pursue.[19]

The Bedouin's native knowledge resulted in keen, and unexpected, methods of survival.

Wilfred Thesiger, considered by some to be the greatest Western desert explorer, went as far as to adopt the customs of his Bedouin companions in order to survive the incredible journeys across the desert. In one instance, Thesiger and his Bedouin companions were trying to convince their camels to drink brackish, disgusting water from a well. Al Auf, his companion, said that the Arabs would consume the undrinkable water mixed with milk if necessary to survive, adding that "if an Arab was really thirsty he would even kill a camel and drink the liquid in its stomach, or ram a stick down its throat and drink the vomit."[20]

In the wilderness, there is no substitute for deep, intimate, firsthand knowledge. If you go to the desert, you consult a Bedouin. If you go to Mount Everest, you work with a Sherpa. You may retire once, but a financial advisor helps hundreds of people retire. You may experience a single IRS audit, but an accountant deals with them every day.

In nearly all of the great, real-life stories of adventure, exploration, and survival, natives are the unsung heroes. Theodore Roosevelt's expedition of the River of Doubt hinged on local natives with an incredible ability to navigate the river and endure the rugged journey that nearly took Roosevelt's life. The great Western explorers in the early twentieth century who traversed the Arabian and Saharan deserts owed their lives to the Bedouins.

When a brand finds itself in unknown territory, there is no substitute for native knowledge. The challenge for brands in an economy that is experiencing exponentially fragmenting knowledge is that you can't internally staff a native in every domain. You must seek out connections with natives in other domains that can be called upon when needed. But it's not effective to find just any native in a given domain. You must find the natives with curated knowledge.

Adaptation Requires Curated Curators

According to the *Oxford Dictionary*, to curate is to "select, organize, and present"[21] information. Historically, a curator—one who has a caretaking role at a museum—was in charge of sifting through enormous numbers of artifacts and pieces of art and selecting which pieces would be presented and how they would be displayed. Today, the term is applied to every domain.

Fundamentally, curation is informed decision making. It is native advice. It is "yes" to this and "no" to that. Curators bring order from chaos. They design knowledge. The great brands don't just design products anymore, they design every aspect of their customers' experience. They look for signal in noise and understand how to present it to the world. Curation is the essential value of many of today's brands. It's elemental to what makes Google and Apple Google and Apple.

In today's noisy marketplace, the value of curation has never been higher. Malcolm Gladwell explains the rising importance of curators in his book *The Tipping Point*, writing, "When people are overwhelmed with information and develop immunity to traditional forms of communication, they turn instead for advice and information to the people in their lives whom they respect, admire, and trust."[22]

To succeed, modern brands must both curate and seek curators. If you are successful, chances are you already curate for your customer to some degree. But to enable your brand to adapt to constantly changing circumstances, you have to "select, organize, and present" the curators inside other domains. You have to curate the experts who not only natively understand their industry but are widely connected to other experts and resources within their domain.

You are not looking for just any expert but for connected experts. You are curating curators and building a network of people with highly effective networks. By creating your network of networks, you are creating shortcuts to immense amounts of information that you can swiftly call upon when needed. Once you have identified highly connected experts who curate their own domains, it's time to connect the dots.

Adaptation Requires Connected Connections

By emphasizing connection over in-house capability, you are institutionalizing flexibility. Sagging economies, market disruption, and unexpected competition don't cut as deeply if you have less to lose. If you are able to combine institutionalized flexibility with an open system that continually gathers as many new perspectives as possible, even in hardship you will be positioned to adapt and thrive in the wilderness.

Mark Parker underscored Nike's commitment to connection in uncertainty, saying, "The biggest sources of opportunity are collaboration and partnership. And today, with digital communication, there is more of that everywhere. We need to expose ourselves to that as a matter of doing business."[23]

Once you have identified domain natives with curated knowledge, it is vital to keep your network accessible and to encourage cross-pollination. In practical terms, you need to create and nurture "the Collective," a curated list of curators across many different domains. We may be a strategic marketing firm, but our Collective is filled with names of scientists, engineers, architects, anthropologists, venture capitalists, and more. We have gone so far as to create a staff position focused solely on building and nurturing the Collective who then consults the team to identify which members best suit particular challenges. It saves us time. It saves us money. It saves us angst. And it makes us more effective.

Competitive advantage for modern brands is less about the ability to do everything and more about the ability to connect to doers. Or, as Malcolm Gladwell put it, "Acquaintances . . . represent a source of social power, and the more acquaintances you have the more powerful you are."[24] The next time your brand is stuck in a life raft in the middle of the Atlantic, if your meal relies on a spear gun manufacturer, you're probably going to starve. But brands that are able to connect a butter knife expert with a floating plastic connoisseur, well, they might just have a chance to live.

MacGyver on the Open Sea

After using every ounce of his strength and will desperately trying to keep his sinking life raft afloat, Steve Callahan gave up. Fifty days of hell on the high seas was enough. It was time to die. As he lay down to give up, the finality of leaving the earth truly sank in. Callahan realized he wasn't ready. In his greatest accomplishment of the ordeal, he got up and managed to patch the tear in the life raft. He called it "the biggest victory of my life."[25]

Callahan knew his only hope was to get the attention of a passing ship. He created a strict routine of scanning the horizon for signs of life every thirty minutes during the day and every time he awoke at night. He also attempted to divine his position based on his limited access to navigation and pure reckoning. Fifty days soon became sixty, which dragged on to seventy. Finally, a break. Callahan began to notice signs of landfall as the dorado fish disappeared and frigate birds appeared overhead.[26]

Callahan's heroics were exhausting but effective. His ordeal wasn't over yet, though. Even as he observed encouraging signs of land, his solar still ripped. Floating hours or even days from land, with his freshwater device irreparably broken, he figured that was the end. He only had three cans of water left. He wrote that his "body and mind were shutting down; it was as if I could feel all the people who had ever been lost at sea around me. I had no more to give."[27]

Adrift on the sea, lasting longer in a life raft than any other human recorded in history, Callahan awaited his end. Until, at last, a fisherman spotted Callahan's strange floating island. The fish guts and human activity that surrounded the life raft had created a little ecosystem, attracting circling birds that caught the fisherman's eye. When the fisherman went to investigate, he found a man barely alive.

By the time he was rescued, Steve Callahan had survived seventy-six days adrift on the sea. He told *The Guardian* that he lost a third of his body weight, and it took him more than six weeks to walk correctly again.[28] Through incredible feats of human ingenuity, Callahan became the only man to ever survive for two and a half months in a six-foot life raft in the middle of the ocean.

Adaptation isn't just a new tool in your toolkit. Adaptation is a way of thinking and a way of operating. Adaptation doesn't require you to overcome uncertainty; it requires you to embrace uncertainty. When you've reached the point at which uncertainty isn't an enemy to be overcome but a condition to be embraced, you're ready to adapt. You're ready to revel.

Armed with the knowledge that uncertainty and ambiguity are the only things we can truly count on and that closed systems die, move your brand to Condition Yellow. Shift your underlying systems from a focus on efficiency to a focus on flexibility, then open those systems to constant streams of new information. Build your Collective by curating curators and connecting them to one another and your needs. Then marvel as your brand turns bicycles and plastic trash into snowmobiles and spear guns.

Survival Tips for Practical Application

No matter how long you've been floating in that life raft, it's never too late to change your mindset, adapt, and live.

Keep in Mind

- Three principles teach us to never rely on old forms of success: Gödel's Incompleteness Theorems, Heisenberg's Uncertainty Principle, and the Second Law of Thermodynamics.
- Two truths will inspire you to action: (1) uncertainty and ambiguity are here to stay and (2) closed systems die.
- Most organizations are built on twentieth-century business concepts, emphasizing efficiency over flexibility and seeking to minimize uncertainty rather than embrace it.

Survival Tips

To navigate The Wild:

- Move your brand to a state of relaxed alertness.
- Seek deep knowledge in the form of domain natives.
- Seek curated knowledge in the form of domain curators.
- Curate your curators into a living list.
- Continually connect your curators to one another and your needs.

Notes

1. Robert Safian, "How CEO Mark Parker Runs Nike to Keep Pace with Rapid Change," *Fast Company*, November 5, 2012, http://www.fastcompany. com/3002642/how-ceo-mark-parker-runs-nike-keep-pace-rapid-change.
2. Steven Callahan, *Adrift: Seventy-six Days Lost at Sea* (Thorndike: Thorndike Press, 1986), 118; Steven Callahan, "Experience: I Was Adrift on a Raft in the Atlantic for 76 Days," *The Guardian*, March 23, 2012, https://www.the guardian.com/lifeandstyle/2012/mar/23/adrift-in-atlantic-76-days.
3. Callahan, *Adrift*, 295.
4. Safian, "How CEO Mark Parker Runs Nike to Keep Pace with Rapid Change."
5. Brett McKay and Kaye McKay, "The Tao of Boyd: How to Master the OODA Loop," *The Art of Manliness*, September 15, 2014, http://www. artofmanliness.com/2014/09/15/ooda-loop/.
6. McKay, "The Tao of Boyd."
7. Panu Raatikainen, "Gödel's Incompleteness Theorems," in *Stanford Encyclopedia of Philosophy*, January 20, 2015, http://plato.stanford.edu/entries/ goedel-incompleteness/.
8. Alok Jha, "What Is Heisenberg's Uncertainty Principle?" *The Guardian*, November 10, 2013, https://www.theguardian.com/science/2013/nov/10/ what-is-heisenbergs-uncertainty-principle.
9. Dave Gray and Thomas Vander Wal, *The Connected Company* (Sebastopol: O'Reilly Media, 2012), 132, https://medium.com/the-connected-company/ wrangling-complexity-8f9fd72dffe1#.svck0zphr.
10. Safian, "How CEO Mark Parker Runs Nike to Keep Pace with Rapid Change."
11. Michael Hendrix, "Ideo: Is Jazz School the Next Great Innovation Incubator?" *Fast Company*, June 17, 2016, https://www.fastcodesign.com/3060997/ideo-is-jazz-school-the-next-great-innovation-incubator.
12. McKay, "The Tao of Boyd."
13. McKay, "The Tao of Boyd."
14. Callahan, *Adrift*, 293–297.
15. Callahan, *Adrift*, 304.
16. Callahan, *Adrift*, 270.
17. Richard Fairburn, "Cooper's Colors: A Simple System for Situational Awareness," *PoliceOne*, August 9, 2010, https://www.policeone.com/police-trainers/ articles/2188253-Coopers-colors-A-simple-system-for-situational-awareness/.

18. McKay, "The Tao of Boyd."

19. Bertram Thomas, *Arabia Felix: Across the Empty Quarter of Arabia* (London: Readers' Union, 1938), 251.

20. Wilfred Thesiger, *Arabian Sands* (Harmondsworth, Middlesex: Penguin Books, 1964), 153.

21. *Oxford Dictionary,* s.v. "Curate," accessed August 5, 2016, http://www.oxforddictionaries.com/us/definition/american_english/curate.

22. Malcolm Gladwell, *The Tipping Point: How Little Things Can Make a Big Difference* (New York: Back Bay Books, 2002), 275.

23. Safian, "How CEO Mark Parker Runs Nike to Keep Pace with Rapid Change."

24. Gladwell, *The Tipping Point*, 54.

25. Callahan, "Experience: I Was Adrift on a Raft in the Atlantic for 76 Days."

26. Callahan, *Adrift*, 302–305.

27. Callahan, "Experience: I was Adrift on a Raft in the Atlantic for 76 Days."

28. Callahan, "Experience: I was Adrift on a Raft in the Atlantic for 76 Days."

CHAPTER 11

Do

Descent was totally unappetizing. The rotten rock, the softening snow, the absence of even tolerable piton cracks only added to our desire to go on. Too much labor, too many sleepless nights, and too many dreams had been invested to bring us this far. We couldn't come back for another try next weekend. To go down now, even if we could have, would be descending to a future marked by one huge question; what might have been? It would not be a matter of living with our fellow man, but simply living with ourselves, with the knowledge that we had had more to give.[1]
—Thomas F. Hornbein, *Everest: The West Ridge*

Breathless, Thomas Hornbein pulled himself up and over the cliff that his climbing partner, Willi Unsoeld, had just masterfully navigated. The altimeter read 27,900 feet. The pair were so close to being the first humans in history to travel across Mount Everest that caution and self-preservation were fading behind pure climbing fervor.

The path they chose proved exceptionally difficult, but they had climbed so far that turning back now might be just as dangerous as remaining. A leaky oxygen tank meant Unsoeld had run out of the precious air in only six hours. Near the top of the world, every movement already felt like pushing a giant redwood through a Louisiana swamp. Without oxygen, the smallest actions now required monumental effort. The pair still had more than one thousand feet to ascend, but they consoled themselves that, without the oxygen tank, at least Unsoeld would be able to climb ten pounds lighter.[2]

As Hornbein and Unsoeld paused on the cliff, trying to regain their breath, they radioed base camp. Unsoeld's status update did not go over well with Jim Whittaker, the first American to summit Mount Everest[3] and their only contact with human life ten thousand feet below. Hornbein and Unsoeld had taken an especially difficult path and left almost no room to go back safely: "no rappel points, Jim, absolutely no rappel points," Unsoeld relayed to Whittaker below, "and we'll probably be getting in pretty late."[4]

Standing on the side of the mountain nearly twenty-eight thousand feet above the earth, there were no good options. The best the climbers could hope for now was to reach the summit before nightfall, then immediately descend the other side in darkness. With a treacherous ascent behind and a nighttime descent ahead, they pushed on.[5]

The Wild may be a force to be reckoned with, but it takes no sides in your internal battle between success and failure. After all is said and done, what you do is the only thing that matters. You can plan for every eventuality, train for every danger, and evaluate every measure of performance. But after the dust has settled, it is what you do or don't do that defines you.

The culmination of everything The Wild has to teach us is found in the moment in which insight meets action. A lost brand can diagnose and rightly understand its place on the descent from fear and drift to inconsistency and savagery. But if the principles of stopping, orienting, and focusing aren't acted upon and the hard decisions behind flow and adaptation aren't made, all is for naught. As branding expert, Steve McKee, put it in *Power Branding*, "strategy without execution is only theory."

Today, in this moment, you have the opportunity to act. And in that decision, you begin to unlock the hidden power of *doing*. Twenty-eight thousand feet above the earth, Thomas Hornbein discovered a similar truth. Layer after layer of specialized clothing and equipment designed

to retain warmth provided a pitiful shield against the mountain's penetrating cold. As Hornbein slipped on multiple mittens and prepared to tie
into yet another rope on his journey up the mountain, he stopped for the
briefest moment to reflect on his actions:

> I snugged the bowline about my waist, feeling satisfaction at the
> ease with which the knot fell together beneath heavily mitted
> hands. This was part of the ritual, experienced innumerable times
> before. . . To weave the knot so smoothly with clumsily mitted
> hands was to assert my confidence, to assert some competence in
> the face of the waiting rock, to accept the challenge.[6]

Hornbein's tiny ritual provided comfort in the most hostile environment on earth. The act, in and of itself, brought courage and familiarity
into a terrifying and utterly unknown place. Thus, doing isn't just about
what you hope to accomplish as a result of your actions, it's about the
benefit of the act of acting itself. Action. Doing. Moving. In and of itself,
movement has power.

Equipped with the knowledge of how lost brands descend from fear
and drift to inconsistency and savagery and an understanding of the path
back to resilience, how do you know where to start? What should your
first action be?

The answer will be different in every case, but Admiral McRaven,
the ninth commander of the United States Special Operations Command,
who oversaw SEAL Team 6 during the Bin Laden raid, provides a valuable hint. In a commencement speech at the University of Texas, the
admiral shared his now-famous advice to young students eager to change
the world: "Start by making your bed."[7] He would go on to explain that
this simple, seemingly insignificant act holds the key to everything else.
With this act, you gain your first sense of pride in a task completed,
encouraging you to create the next link in a chain of tasks completed and
reinforcing the fact that "little things in life matter."[8] And at the end of the
day, even if you've failed, you come home to a made bed.

So where, exactly, do you begin in your journey from lost to resilient? You start small.

Tom Antram, president and CEO of French Funerals & Cremations, started small by implementing what he described as branding's version of the broken windows theory. French is New Mexico's largest and oldest family-owned funeral service company and a longtime client of my firm. Founded by Chester T. French in 1907, the company has a long and proud tradition of caring for families in their deepest moments of need. But it, and the entire death care industry, had a problem.

Antram outlined the mounting challenges facing his industry in an interview with my firm, explaining that companies like his had ignored dramatic changes in customer preferences for many years. Historically, traditional funeral services (including burial) were the core revenue stream in death care. But the higher cost of burial, Americans' increasing mobility, and a cultural shift away from formal religion correlated with a rising demand for cremation and nontraditional services. Because cremation revenue is significantly lower than that of burial, the industry found itself in a pinch. Most providers, including French, initially responded by sticking their heads in the sand.

By the late 1990s, the cremation trend was starting to affect the bottom line, and French had to do something. But like many businesses, it had become too comfortable in its position as the market leader and struggled with complacency inside the company. As Antram put it, "We had people more skilled at avoiding work than performing." He told an incredible story of dealing with employees who literally hid from work, and he later learned that they regularly joked that the only thing that could get you fired at a company built on caring was to do something immoral. French knew how to graciously take care of grieving families, but the company's operations were a mess.

To make matters worse, the organization had no formalized internal processes; as other industries modernized through online platforms and electronic records, death care lagged far behind. Shrinking revenue, profit pressure, and an internal culture of institutionalized complacency created a real uphill battle for French. To begin the process of addressing the company's core problems, Antram said that the only way they could tackle their biggest challenges was to start small.

Antram explained that French first embraced branding's version of the broken windows theory. The theory, made famous by former New York City mayor Rudy Giuliani and police commissioner William Bratton in the 1990s, focused on addressing minor crime in the belief that the effect would prevent more serious crime. According to *Encyclopedia Britannica Online*, the theory is built on the idea that "disorder causes crime, and crime causes further disorder and crime."[9] If "crime emanated from disorder and that if disorder were eliminated, then serious crimes would not occur."

Based on the theory, Bratton and Giuliani pursued a strategy of clamping down on minor crimes and misdemeanors, focusing on panhandling, street prostitution, public drinking, and more. As a result, during Bratton's tenure as police commissioner, New York City felonies declined by nearly 40 percent, and homicides were reduced by nearly half.[10]

French's leadership believed that in order to make the fundamental changes needed to pivot in a quickly changing marketplace, they had to start by getting the smallest things right. They began with a sweeping effort focused on process and metrics. The effort included a multiyear quality initiative that defined internal processes and outlined employee performance measures.

The initiative resulted in the documentation of more than four hundred processes, enough for Antram to admit that they "may have" gone a bit overboard. But the course correction was necessary. The initiative also resulted in new and improved methods by which employee performance could be measured against industry standards. And with that knowledge came an even more difficult challenge: holding employees and leadership accountable.

By this point, French had taken two important steps toward course correction, admitting it had a problem and orienting itself through internal measurement. Now that it was armed with the knowledge it needed to act, it entered into the phase in which most brands fall down. It was time to do something.

Brands struggle with taking action for the same reason we all do: no matter the purpose, humans don't like change. Dr. Christopher J. Anderson has made studying decision making his life's work. In his study titled *The Psychology of Doing Nothing*, Dr. Anderson describes what he calls "decision avoidance" as a "tendency to avoid making a choice by postponing it or by seeking an easy way out that involves no action or no change."[11]

Anderson goes on to explain that decision avoidance is rooted in four common psychological phenomena: choice deferral, status quo bias, omission bias, and inaction inertia. These phenomena all reflect a fundamental truth about the human experience: people simply don't want things to change.

Choice deferral means that people tend to postpone choices when uncertainty is high until they are able to understand the process in which that uncertainty will be reduced.[12] It is a form of delay and can be both positive and negative. In its positive form, it is a natural process for vetting options. In its most negative form, choice deferral is just an excuse to avoid making a decision.

Status quo bias explains how most people, most of the time, prefer for things to stay the same. We observe this phenomenon in our consulting practice every day. Many brands will admit they are lost and perhaps even invest in the steps necessary to orient the organization and gather the data they need to make informed decisions. But when it's time to act, they hesitate.

Often in our practice, we work with brands that like to talk about their problems, but when it's time to do something about it, they are content to die a slow death. Or worse, they halfheartedly dip their toes into the tough business of turning the brand around when they never had a true intention of following through.

Related but different are the phenomena known as omission bias and inaction inertia. Omission bias characterizes the fallacy that inaction is somehow safer or more moral than taking action. It is a form of self-imposed paralysis hiding behind the lie that inaction is not a choice.

Inaction inertia is a fascinating phenomenon in which the decision to not take action on an initial opportunity decreases the likelihood of taking action on subsequent opportunities, regardless of their merit.[13] Basically, if you don't act when you first get the chance, you're less likely to act the next time.

Inaction inertia usually rears its ugly head in the form of perpetual planning. This is when brands continually explore the possibilities of how they might solve a particular problem but never pull the trigger. President Dwight D. Eisenhower, a former WWII general and leader of the Allied armies, famously quipped that "plans are useless, but planning is indispensable."[14] I might add a corollary: planning is indispensable, but perpetual planning is deadly.

Dr. Anderson's concept of decision avoidance is helpful in understanding the different ways we all get trapped in the status quo. When facing the choice to act, we need to know that we are hardwired not to. Nothing inside us wants to do what we need to do. It was for this reason that during Hornbein and Unsoeld's attempt to be the first humans to traverse Mount Everest, the more they could do to make the status quo uncomfortable, the more likely they would be to press on.

As Hornbein heard Unsoeld wrapping up his radio update to base camp ten thousand feet below, the realization of what he'd said finally sank in: "no rappel points, Jim, absolutely no rappel points." But instead of Unsoeld's words filling Hornbein with fear, they filled him with determination. With the highest peak in the world within reach, the seriousness of the situation only brought focus to his efforts. Hornbein later wrote of his moment of self-reflection, "That we couldn't go down only made easier that which we really wanted to do. That we might not get there was scarcely conceivable."[15] Hornbein and Unsoeld overcame their desire to give up by cutting off their own escape.

Once the French Funerals & Cremations management team had in place the internal performance measures and documented processes it required to make informed decisions, it acted. The company went through the painful process of installing accountability across the organization, resulting in a three-year period in which the company experienced 75 percent turnover. Commenting on that difficult period, Tom Antram said, "Some of our team did not make the transition; but those that have are performing at levels none of us thought possible."[16]

During the same time period, French restructured its leadership team by thinning out certain areas and bringing focus to others. But Antram emphasized that tightening the ship and bringing clarity and accountability to internal performance didn't come at the expense of culture. In fact, he stressed the opposite. Speaking about the special pressures of working in death care, Antram said, "The emotional toll of serving others can be immense. We need to provide the resources to keep those individuals balanced both emotionally and physically."[17]

He went on to explain that protecting employees and fostering a healthy culture go hand in hand with financial controls and accountability. That belief inspired French to create the Grief Resource Center, a counseling service created specifically to support those who have experienced a death. It also led to an internal focus on wellness programs to encourage employees to be healthy not only spiritually and emotionally but also physically.

Once French had stopped, oriented, and taken action internally, it refocused on the changing marketplace and its place in it. Antram identified French's need to adapt, starting by admitting to himself that "doing things the way we've always done them doesn't work." Antram said that today's consumer expects more and that to survive in the death care industry, French had to "serve a greater number of families, increase our reach, and diversify."

The company's first foray into diversification, a cremation subbrand called Aspen Cremation, was a flop. According to Antram, Aspen had been created to serve the growing market of people who opted for cremation but didn't want the full-service offerings French was known for. But what started with good intentions quickly turned into "a little French."

Full service was in the company's blood, and Aspen never made a profit, resulting in the decision to shut it down in 2008.

The false start didn't discourage the French team. Instead, they accepted their lesson in humility and, as their next move toward diversification, pursued acquisition of a company that provided funeral services for pets. The decision proved prescient, as the service expectations of the acquired company's customer base jived with the French culture, resulting in happy customers and a new, sustainable line of business.

French then built on its newfound success by relaunching the cremation subbrand under a new name. This time, however, the company intentionally limited its own leadership involvement in the establishment of service guidelines, allowing the new venture to be what it was intended to be without the full-service expectation of its parent company. The pet funeral service operation and cremation subbrand now represent the company's highest-margin business lines.

Diversification was one thing, but reevaluating the relevance of the core French Funeral brand was another. In the face of dramatic cultural changes in funeral preferences, French knew that it couldn't continue down the same path. To orient itself to the changing market, French recruited twelve other leading funeral homes from across the United States to share the significant costs of conducting a comprehensive (and unusual) nationwide study about death.

The study had more than 3,000 participants and explored every aspect of the way people think about and deal with death, from service preferences to belief in the afterlife and more. It even plumbed details into seemingly unrelated preferences like eating habits and online behaviors.

The results of the study were revealing, confirming what many in the industry felt but couldn't articulate. A large and growing segment of the population not only preferred cremation over burial and nontraditional services over traditional but wanted to interface with the industry digitally.

The study reinforced what French had suspected for years. If it wanted to continue to thrive, it must redefine not only its position in the marketplace but the company's own perspective on its core competency. Antram called this shift a recommitment to being a service-oriented company. By emphasizing French's definition of its core competency as service, it freed the organization to encourage change among its customers rather than fight it, allowing French to adapt, as Antram put it, to "cultural preferences regarding how people choose to honor a loved one's life."

French focused on its "why," summing up its purpose in the singular concept of "ease." No matter what method a person wanted to use to honor a loved one, French existed to ease the way. And well beyond the funeral service itself, French's purpose is to ease everyone involved— loved ones, grieving family and friends, and the community at large— through the heavy process of grief. This focus opened up worlds of possibility to French.

French was now in a position to become a driver of the very industry disruption it had resisted for years. With the discovery that a large and growing market segment preferred to arrange funerals digitally, French launched and became the first investor in a tech start-up that would open up the industry to digital collaboration with its customers and enable funeral arrangements to be made from anywhere in the world. More than a dozen other funeral homes joined French in pioneering this new effort, which is now dramatically enhancing their ability to "ease" their customers through the grieving process.

French's efforts also culminated in a breakthrough integrated marketing campaign. Built on the company's service focus, French repositioned its brand to appeal to a younger, digitally minded consumer and used an online campaign to target a spectrum of consumers at every level of need. Billboards served as top-of-mind awareness drivers with simple messages like "YODO," "Leave Well," and "Carpe di End." Ongoing storytelling events and sophisticated content marketing and social media rounded out the effort.

As a result of these initiatives, French bucked industry trends by generating significant year-over-year revenue growth. It turned sagging brand awareness and preference measures around and achieved higher and more consistent customer satisfaction scores than leadership ever thought possible. Antram summed up the company's transformation by saying, "We are serving a greater number of families, with consistent customer satisfaction scores, and with greater financial impact," adding, "We used to be on the defensive. Now we're on the offensive."[18] Not bad for a brand that started with broken windows.

Victory

Hornbein and Unsoeld left the cliff more determined then when they arrived. The pair's ascent of the west ridge was inordinately slow but effective. By three in the afternoon, they had been climbing for more than eight hours. They stopped to refuel on tasteless, frozen snacks out of a sense of duty. The mountain was calling.[19]

Even as the pair reached higher altitudes, their strength seemed to grow. They were now within four hundred feet of the summit. The snow turned to rock, so Hornbein and Unsoeld packed up their over-boots and crampons in exchange for cleated rubber soles. Hornbein's oxygen ran out, but he didn't mind. He felt like he could run the final stretch.[20]

The climbers were so close now. Unsoeld suddenly stopped, confusing Hornbein as he followed behind. Later, Hornbein wrote, "With a feeling of disbelief I looked up. . . . It was 6:15. The sun's rays sheered horizontally across the summit. We hugged each other as tears welled up, ran down across our oxygen masks, and turned to ice."[21]

The pair's nighttime descent was treacherous but not fatal. The fierce mountain would claim all of Unsoeld's toes, which had to be amputated due to severe frostbite. But even the rugged west ridge and foolish night-time descent couldn't stop Hornbein and Unsoeld, who returned to base camp hours later, having become the first humans to travel up one side of

Mount Everest and down the other. It was a feat that would later be called the greatest achievement in Everest history.[22]

Doing isn't a matter of exact timing. Doing doesn't rely on perfect information. Doing never requires more money or resources. Doing is up to you. You are hardwired for inaction and inertia. You don't want to *do*. But in the midst of the terror and loneliness that mark much of the wilderness, doing is exactly what must be done.

Wherever your lost brand finds itself in the descent from fear to savagery, remember that doing isn't just a matter of achieving your ultimate goal. Doing is a feat in and of itself. Action begets action. Doing inspires confidence and dispels negativity.

Dr. Anderson's decision-avoidance behaviors outline all the reasons you will resist doing. It is up to you to be aware of your natural tendencies, overcome your own limitations, and inspire those around you to action. As Admiral McRaven learned from his extensive career as a Navy SEAL, big achievements start with small actions. If your brand is lost in the wilderness, don't start your journey toward resilience by trying to build an airplane and a runway. Look for the smallest opportunity for success, then act. Once you "make your bed," you can change the world.

Survival Tips for Practical Application

Branding isn't just planning and strategy, branding is doing. Now you are equipped with an understanding of how and why brands descend into savagery and outfitted with a detailed map that will help you navigate your way back toward resilience—and now is the time to act.

Keep in Mind

- Doing is the culmination of everything The Wild has to teach us.
- Doing, in and of itself, is valuable.
- Humans are hardwired to avoid change.
- Decision avoidance is made up of four parts, including choice deferral, status quo bias, omission bias, and inaction inertia.

Survival Tips

To navigate The Wild:

- Document your brand's struggles with doing.
- Start small.
- Don't wait for the right circumstance. Act now.

Notes

1. Thomas F. Hornbein, *Everest: The West Ridge* (Seattle: Mountaineers, 1998), 163–164.
2. Hornbein, *Everest*, 162.
3. Ron Judd, "In the Spirit of His Home State, Jim Whittaker Defined Daring," *The Seattle Times*, April 12, 2013, http://www.seattletimes.com/pacific-nw-magazine/in-the-spirit-of-his-home-state-jim-whittaker-defined-daring/.
4. Hornbein, *Everest*, 162–164.
5. Hornbein, *Everest*, 163.
6. Hornbein, *Everest*, 158–159.
7. "Adm. McRaven Urges Graduates to Find Courage to Change the World," *UT News*, May 16, 2014, http://news.utexas.edu/2014/05/16/mcraven-urges-graduates-to-find-courage-to-change-the-world.
8. "Adm. McRaven Urges Graduates to Find Courage to Change the World."
9. Adam J. McKee, "Broken Windows Theory," *Encyclopedia Britannica Online*, accessed August 20, 2016, https://www.britannica.com/topic/broken-windows-theory.
10. McKee, "Broken Windows Theory."
11. Christopher J. Anderson, *The Psychology of Doing Nothing: Forms of Decision Avoidance Result from Reason and Emotion*, PDF, American Psychological Association, http://homepages.se.edu/cvonbergen/files/2013/01/The-Psychology-of-Doing-Nothing_Forms-of-Decision-Avoidance-Result-from-Reason-and-Emotion.pdf.
12. Igor Kopylov, Choice Deferral and Ambiguity Aversion." PDF. Theoretical Economics, 4, no. 2 (June 2016), 199–225, https://webfiles.uci.edu/ikopylov/www/files/deferral.pdf.
13. Orit E. Tykocinski, Thane S. Pittman, and Erin E. Tuttle, "Inaction Inertia: Foregoing Future Benefits as a Result of an Initial Failure to Act," *Journal of Personality and Social Psychology* 68, no. 5 (May 1995), 783–803.

14. "Eisenhower Quotes," National Archives and Records Administration, accessed September 3, 2016, https://www.eisenhower.archivechives and Records Administrations.gov/all_about_ike/quotes.html.

15. Hornbein, *Everest*, 164.

16. Tom Antram (President of French Funerals), interview by Jonathan David Lewis, French Funerals-Cremations Headquarters, August 22, 2016.

17. Antram (President of French Funerals), interview by Jonathan David Lewis, French Funerals-Cremations Headquarters.

18. Antram (President of French Funerals), interview by Jonathan David Lewis, French Funerals-Cremations Headquarters.

19. Hornbein, *Everest*, 165.

20. Hornbein, *Everest*, 166.

21. Hornbein, *Everest*, 167.

22. David Roberts, ed., *Points Unknown: The Greatest Adventure Writing of the Twentieth Century* (New York: W. W. Norton, 2002), 487.

Conclusion

One gives freely, yet grows all the richer; another withholds what he should give, and only suffers want.[1]

—Proverbs 11:24

Welcome to the wilderness. You have journeyed through the heart of darkness, watched as even the strongest brands fall victim to fear and savagery, and learned how to climb back up the mountain to resilience. You are equipped for success and ready to act.

After all is said and done, one truth undergirds them all: the only wild you have control over is The Wild within. You have no influence over the next economic downturn, competitive move, or industry disruption. The responsibility to overcome The Wild within your brand, your team, and yourself, however, is in your hands.

When many automatic psychological and physiological processes in you are hardwired to act against your ultimate best interest, you quickly discover that resilience is built on overcoming self. Fear is overcome through courage, drift and inconsistency through focus, and savagery through alignment. Each solution is a form of selflessness.

One of the most important and least understood forces in the wilderness is the will to live. In example after example, a person or group will be confronted by an impossible situation, give in to despair, then mysteriously rally and find salvation. This will to live is rarely rooted in a simple desire to live but often in a desire to live *for* something. It is others centric. The will to live thrives on purpose that is outside of self.

Sometimes it is family, other times it is God, and still others it is a sense of duty and greater good.

Don't confuse selflessness with a lack of self-interest. Jesus didn't famously say, "Love your neighbor." He said, "Love your neighbor as yourself."[2] Self-interest is healthy and necessary to survive in the wilderness. But selfishness is the quickest route to savagery.

When business leaders talk about culture, they are really just saying they wish their team had a healthy sense of selflessness. As any expert in team building will tell you, the first step toward building a team is diminishing an individual's sense of "I" in favor of "we." The Navy SEALS have famously built their entire training program on the premise that they must destroy self before they can build an effective team. The traditions of BUD/S training, including Hell Week, sleep deprivation, hypothermic conditions, and mind-breaking toil are all purposely constructed to destroy a sense of self and rebuild a soldier's purpose around the good of the team. The result? Regardless of an aspiring soldier's physical condition, most can't make it through.

The Navy SEALS's training program has a 75 percent dropout rate[3] for the same reason Dr. John Leach's 10–80–10 theory postulates that 90 percent of people are ill equipped to navigate survival situations: we are not built to be selfless. When you look at all of the iconic brands of the last century, they share an uncommon ability to focus on others by reinventing themselves to meet the market's ever-changing needs. Nike disrupts its own products. LEGO rediscovered what its customers want. Even Steve Jobs, infamous for his destructive ego, had a counterintuitive and draconian focus on his customers.

In the daily minutiae of communications, great branding is still selfless branding. The most effective marketing gives before it gets. Whether you offer a feeling through a smile or a tear, or you improve someone's life through education, all great marketing gives before it expects to get. Nike inspires, Lowe's informs, and Geico entertains. Great brands even build generosity into their operations, from REI's return policy and Zappos's no-rush phone calls to Starbucks's commitment to getting your drink right.

When a brand communicates, consumers implicitly understand that self-interest is baked into the equation. The company must benefit from the transaction; otherwise, it goes out of business. What is unexpected, however, is for a brand to have enough faith in itself and its customer that it places the needs of others first. As more than a decade of my company's research and the latest in survival psychology show us, the brands that give before they get navigate the wilderness with resilience. The selfish turn savage.

If you exist for you and you alone, you will die in the wilderness. The Wild isn't your enemy. You are your enemy. Self is the chief obstacle between you and resilience, and it represents your greatest challenge as you work to overcome fear, find focus, and defeat savagery. To survive, you must let go of the external battle and engage with your internal battle. It is the ability to navigate The Wild within that separates the good from the great and the lost from the found.

Welcome to the wilderness, where the last become first, the first become last, and "success" is spelled "s-e-l-f-l-e-s-s."

Notes

1. *English Standard Version,* Proverbs 11:24.
2. "Luke 10:27," *Bible Hub,* accessed August 1, 2016, http://biblehub.com/luke/10–27.htm.
3. Jeff Kraus, "Hell Week," *Navy Seals,* accessed September 10, 2016, http://navyseals.com/nsw/hell-week-0/.

About the Author

Jonathan David Lewis is a leading expert on shaping brands that can survive—and thrive—in today's tough, uncertain world.

As partner and strategy director at McKee Wallwork + Company, Jonathan led his firm to be recognized by industry purveyor *Advertising Age* as a national leader in branding and marketing, winning the Southwest Small Agency of the Year, national B2B Campaign of the Year, and national Best Places to Work awards.

A branding and business strategist, Jonathan honed his skills during the lean years of the Great Recession, helping brands navigate today's unforgiving new business paradigms. Jonathan's opinions are highly sought by numerous business and marketing publications, including *Forbes*, *Digiday*, and *Advertising Age*, where he explores the factors that lead to stalled growth and the principles proven to help companies navigate the ambiguities and dangers of the brand wilderness.

References

Anderson, Christopher J. *The Psychology of Doing Nothing: Forms of Decision Avoidance Result from Reason and Emotion*. PDF. Washington, DC: American Psychological Association, 2003

Borders Group 2000 Annual Report. PDF. BGI, 2000.

Buxton, William J., ed. *Harold Innis and the North: Appraisals and Contestations*. Montreal & Kingston: McGill-Queen's University Press, 2013.

Callahan, Steven. *Adrift: Seventy-Six Days Lost at Sea*. Thorndike: Thorndike Press, 1986.

Collins, Jim. *Good to Great: Why Some Companies Make the Leap . . . and Others Don't*. New York: Harper Business, 2001.

Csikszentmihalyi, Mihaly. *Good Business: Leadership, Flow, and the Making of Meaning*. New York: Penguin Books, 2004.

Dahlke, Josh. "One Wrong Step." *Outdoor Life*, April 2016, 38–43.

Davidson, Art. *Minus 148°: First Winter Ascent of Mt. McKinley*. 3rd ed. Seattle: Mountaineers, 1999.

Desimone, Robert. Mcgovern.mit.edu. June 22, 2016. https://mcgovern.mit.edu/principal-investigators/robert-desimone.

Fears, J. Wayne. *The Pocket Outdoor Survival Guide: The Ultimate Guide for Short-Term Survival*. New York: Skyhorse, 2011.

Fitzpatrick, Brad. "Your Brain on Survival: Here's What Happens When the Body Shifts into Survival Mode, and How You Can Stay in Control." *Outdoor Life*, 223, no. 3, April 2016, 47.

Fletcher, Colin. *The Man Who Walked through Time*. New York: Vintage Books, 1989.

Gerstner, Louis V., Jr. *Who Says Elephants Can't Dance? Inside IBM's Historic Turnaround*. New York: Harper Business, 2002.

Gladwell, Malcolm. *The Tipping Point: How Little Things Can Make a Big Difference*. New York: Back Bay Books, 2002.

Gossage, Bobbie, ed. "Howard Schultz on How To Lead a Turnaround," *Inc.*, April 1, 2011, http://www.inc.com/magazine/20110401/howard-schultz-on-how-to-lead-a-turnaround.html.

Gray, Dave, and Thomas Vander Wal. *The Connected Company*. Sebastopol: O'Reilly Media, 2012.

Hornbein, Thomas F. *Everest: The West Ridge*. Seattle: Mountaineers, 1998.

John Boyd Compendium. *A Discourse on Winning and Losing: Patterns of Conflict*. PDF. Defense and the National Interest, December 6, 2007.

Junger, Sebastian. *The Perfect Storm: A True Story of Men against the Sea*. New York: W. W. Norton & Company, 2009.

Kane, Joe. *Running the Amazon*. New York: Vintage Books, 1990.

Kelvens, Carissa. *Fear and Anxiety*. Northridge: California State University, 1997. Accessed August 7, 2016, http://www.csun.edu/~vcpsy00h/students/fear.htm.

Kopylov, Igor. "Choice Deferral and Ambiguity Aversion." PDF. Theoretical Economics, 4, no. 2, June 2016, 199–225.

Krakauer, Jon. *Eiger Dreams: Ventures among Men and Mountains*. Guilford: Lyons Press, 2009.

Krebs, Natalie. "The Crash: The Sole Survivor of a Remote Plane Wreck Rescues Herself." *Outdoor Life*, April 2016, 43–45.

Lagace, Martha. "Gerstner: Changing Culture at IBM—Lou Gerstner Discusses Changing the Culture at IBM." HBS Working Knowledge. December 9, 2002. http://hbswk.hbs.edu/archive/3209.html.

"Lou Gerstner's Turnaround Tales at IBM." Wharton University of Pennsylvania (audio blog), December 18, 2002. http://knowledge.wharton.upenn.edu/article/lou-gerstners-turnaround-tales-at-ibm/.

Mark, Gloria, Shamsi T. Iqbal, Mary Czerwinski, Paul Johns, and Akane Sano. "Neurotics Can't Focus: An in Situ Study of Online Multitasking in the Workplace." 2016. Accessed July 10, 2016. http://www.ics. uci.edu/~gmark/Home_page/Research_files/CHI%2016%20Multi-tasking%20and%20Focus.pdf.

McKee, Steve. *When Growth Stalls: How It Happens, Why You're Stuck, and What to Do about It*. San Francisco: Jossey-Bass, 2009.

Millard, Candice. *The River of Doubt: Theodore Roosevelt's Darkest Journey*. New York: Anchor Books, 2006.

McRaven, William H. "Adm. McRaven Urges Graduates to Find Courage to Change the World." *UT News*. May 16, 2014. http://news.utexas.edu/ 2014/05/16/mcraven-urges-graduates-to-find-courage-to-change-the-world.

Perkins, Dennis N. T. *Leading at the Edge: Leadership Lessons from the Extraordinary Saga of Shackleton's Antarctic Expedition*. New York: Amacom, 2000.

Perlman, Howard. "Specific Heat Capacity of Water." USGS. May 2, 2016. http://water.usgs.gov/edu/heat-capacity.html.

Raatikainen, Panu. "Gödel's Incompleteness Theorems." In *Stanford Encyclopedia of Philosophy*, January 20, 2015. http://plato.stanford. edu/entries/goedel-incompleteness/.

Read, Piers Paul. *Alive: Sixteen Men, Seventy-Two Days, and Insurmountable Odds—the Classic Adventure of Survival in the Andes*. New York: Harper Perennial, 2005.

Roberts, David, ed. *Points Unknown: The Greatest Adventure Writing of the Twentieth Century*. New York: W. W. Norton, 2002.

Romero, Jessie. "Economic History: The Rise and Fall of Circuit City." 2013, 31–33. Accessed July 25, 2016. https://www.rich mondfed.org/~/media/richmondfedorg/publications/research/econ_ focus/2013/q3/pdf/economic_history.pdf.

Schultz, Howard, and Joanne Gordon. Introduction. In *Onward: How Starbucks Fought for Its Life without Losing Its Soul*, Xii–Xv. New York: Rodale, 2011.

Scott, Robert Falcon. *Journals: Captain Scott's Last Expedition*. Edited by Max Jones. Oxford: Oxford University Press, 2006.

Search and Rescue Survival Training. PDF. Washington, DC: Department of the Air Force.

Shackleton, Ernest. *South: The Endurance Expedition*. New York: Signet, 1999.

Swenson, Rand. Chapter 9-Limbic System. In *Review of Clinical and Functional Neuroscience-Swenson*, 2006. Accessed August 5, 2016. http://www.dartmouth.edu/%7Erswenson/NeuroSci/chapter_9.html.

Taylor, Michael Ray. *Cave Passages: Roaming the Underground Wilderness*. New York: Vintage Books, 1997.

Thesiger, Wilfred. *Arabian Sands*. Harmondsworth, London: Penguin Books, 1964.

Thomas, Bertram. *Arabia Felix: Across the Empty Quarter of Arabia*. London: Readers' Union, 1938.

Tykocinski, Orit E., Thane S. Pittman, and Erin E. Tuttle. "Inaction Inertia: Foregoing Future Benefits as a Result of an Initial Failure to Act." *Journal of Personality and Social Psychology*, 68, no. 5, May 1995, 783–803.

Wiseman, John 'Lofty'. *SAS Survival Handbook: The Ultimate Guide to Surviving Anywhere*. 3rd ed. New York: William Morrow, 2014.

Zuckoff, Mitchell. *Lost in Shangri-La: A True Story of Survival, Adventure, and the Most Incredible Rescue Mission of World War II*. New York: HarperCollins, 2011.

Index